"This well-considered series of essays, bringing Saint Benedict's Rule into dialogue with contemporary attitudes and issues, is both instructive and entertaining. Each essay is thought-provoking, honest, and challenging. They are also powerful and contemporary expositions of basic monastic values."

—Michael Casey, OCSO
Author of *The Road to Eternal Life: Reflections on the Prologue of Benedict's Rule*

"Pick up this book and you'll find yourself immediately engaged in a conversation, at times inspired or nodding in wholehearted agreement, at other times vehemently disagreeing, and at other times laughing or smiling at its humor. As such, it is a great conversation starter for monastic communities, oblates, and faith sharing groups."

—Colleen Maura McGrane, OSB
Vocation Director
Benedictine Sisters of Perpetual Adoration
Clyde, Missouri

"Perfect conversation partners—St. Benedict and his self-styled curmudgeon disciple, Terrence Kardong! Readers seeking wisdom will find themselves drawn into exchanges on both contemporary and perennial issues facing monastics and others committed to living well in community. Who can escape concerns about mutual presence and mutual assistance, the value of silence, power dynamics, the good uses of electronic stuff, and what not to wear, as well as the dozen other practical topics in this essay collection? The author's opinions will evoke yours."

—Mary Collins, OSB
Mount St. Scholastica
Atchison, Kansas

Dan,
Thanks for being such a
great example to other
Catholic men.
Merry Christmas! *Jay*
12-14-12

Conversation
with Saint Benedict

The Rule in Today's World

Terrence G. Kardong, OSB

LITURGICAL PRESS
Collegeville, Minnesota

www.litpress.org

Cover design by David Manahan, OSB. "Saint Benedict of the Great Plains," Assumption Abbey, Richardton, North Dakota. Sculpture by Raymond Rogers. Photo by Elias Thienpont, OSB.

1   2   3   4   5   6   7   8

Library of Congress Cataloging-in-Publication Data

Kardong, Terrence.
    Conversation with Saint Benedict : The rule in today's world / Terrence Kardong.
        p.   cm.
    ISBN 978-0-8146-3419-6 — ISBN 978-0-8146-3420-2 (e-book)
    1. Benedict, Saint, Abbot of Monte Cassino. Regula.   2. Spiritual life—Christianity.   I. Title.

BX3004.Z5K343   2012
255'.106—dc23   2011051549

Contents

Preface

Conversation with Saint Benedict is a book of essays. The saint, of course, is long dead, but we can still dialogue with him because he left us a written testament to his monastic thinking, now known as The Rule of St. Benedict. In effect, we can ask Benedict about the monastic life by studying his Rule. We can also ask him questions about certain aspects of our own culture, but these latter, of course, have to be approached indirectly. The obvious reason is that Benedict lived in the sixth century, over 1500 years ago. Nonetheless, we can deduce his attitude toward modern issues by a careful study of what he has to say about the monastic issues of his own day.

The present group of essays began with a set of talks on contemporary questions such as the use of electronic media. In those talks I was mainly trying to get at features of our culture I find difficult and troubling. In short, I am criticizing some things about life as we now find it. But as I added to that particular series of essays I began to feel a twinge of guilt because I could easily have been accused of "culture bashing." The reader could readily come to the conclusion that I am alienated from my own times and culture.

That is not really the case. While I am a Benedictine monk who has left the "world" to live a secluded life, I did not do so (fifty years ago!) because I hate the world. In fact, I am very interested in the world I live in and I try my best to know what is going on in it. Moreover, even though I know there are some things about contemporary culture that are rather troubling and even ugly, I also think there are some features of the Rule of Benedict that can be called into question. In addition, I think modern monks have distorted some of Benedict's teachings. Therefore I wrote a series of parallel essays dealing with the second category as well, namely, what could stand improvement in monasticism, ancient and modern.

My method in all these essays is essentially to first present the problem, whether in modern or monastic culture, and then propose some solutions to the problem. So, for example, after I pose a problem in modern culture I follow up with material from the Rule of Benedict that I think can contribute to a solution. Conversely, when dealing with the elements of the Rule or monastic practice that I find wanting, I first give the monastic theory and/or practice and then present my own suggestions for improvement. Since I am living in the twenty-first century, these suggestions stem from my own culture.

What are my qualifications for such an enterprise? What do I know about modern life? This is not an idle question since I live in a remote monastery and do not move about much in secular life. I do a certain amount of traveling for business, but this mostly takes me to other monasteries. Yet no matter how much monks claim to have "fled from the world," we ourselves come from the world. And the world also has a way of following us into the monastery. For example, in my own monastery we make no pretense of excluding the mass media. We watch television, we use the Internet, and we take a fair number of current journals—far more than the average household! So we know what is going on.

Regarding the Rule of Benedict I am not just a casual observer. As a Benedictine monk I am bound to follow it as a living rule for life. Granted, we have modified it in some important ways, but it is still our basic life program. But beyond that I am a scholar who spends much of his time studying the sixth-century Rule of Benedict. I have invested a good deal of the past thirty years into probing the Rule for its meaning. That means both exegesis and hermeneutics: I try to determine what the Rule meant when it was written, and I also try to meditate on what it can mean for us today. A book like the present one is primarily aimed at the hermeneutical enterprise. I will not spend much time with detailed exegetical examination of the ancient text.

By now it should be obvious to the prospective reader that this is not primarily a scholarly book. In fact, I will not provide any bibliographical references to other scholarly works. I might mention other interesting literature in passing, but I will not examine it in any depth. The focus here is on practical issues and practical solutions. These issues may be fairly subtle ones of the spiritual life that will demand theological answers. Nevertheless, I will not engage in any extended theoretical discussion.

Besides being mainly practical, these essays will be somewhat opinionated. I will not take any pains to disguise my own views of matters, whether of present-day affairs or of the monastic ethos. I will only write about what I care about, and I do so in order to exert some influence. What other reason is there to write? I know full well that my jabs at the modern climate, say, "rant radio," will not change anything. Still, somebody has to fight back! As far as the monks go, I also know that my criticisms of their customs, for example the impractical clothing of Benedictine men, will hardly convince many monks to change. But I don't want to depart the world, monastic or secular, without saying my piece.

Assumption Abbey, Richardton, North Dakota
3 March 2011

Chapter One

Laughter and Tears

St. Benedict and the Entertainment Culture

Entertainment Culture

The term "entertainment culture" may not be familiar to the listener or reader. It does not refer to a certain segment of society such as the broadcast industry, but to *all* of our society. My thesis here is that our whole civilization has gradually become immersed in entertainment. In some ways entertainment, which traditionally was meant as a respite from the wear and tear of ordinary existence, has now become the "default mode" of life for us.

No doubt this strange development is partly the result of technology. Our brilliant discoveries and inventions have eliminated a good deal of the drudge work that occupied the average person for most of history. If you are old enough you may remember the predictions of the social scientists who told us that within a few years we would have a lot of leisure time on our hands. For some people that time has come. Of course, others still have to work at two or three jobs to put food on the table or to put the kids through college. But for many people the question now is how to fill up the time between rising and bedtime. The answer to that question, again for many, not for everybody, is the mass media. Many people now watch television for hours a day; others listen to the radio all day long (mostly while multitasking). And many now use the Internet for leisure. The result is that the media are entrusted with the job of keeping us entertained.

Perhaps it would be good at this point to venture a definition of the word entertainment. One of the many meanings given us by Webster is that entertainment is something pleasant to amuse us or distract us. Now of course not everything on radio or television has precisely that purpose. There are serious programs that mean to stimulate our minds with commentary on the real world and its problems. Moreover, some of the offerings in the media can be described as art in the formal sense, which is never something that merely amuses or distracts. Still, I would contend that most of what we now find in the media can be included under the heading of entertainment. Granted, not all entertainment is bad for us. Our mental health requires that we not be serious all the time. We need relaxation and respite from the cares of life, and we cannot tax our brains too much with hard material. Even the Desert Father Antony sometimes used to relax with his disciples. When rebuked by a "philosopher" for his frivolous behavior he replied that the bow that is kept continually strung soon loses its power.

Nevertheless, as I already indicated, the proper role of relaxation is to serve as a short break from a life of work. When entertainment becomes the whole of life or takes up too much of our time we become shallow and frivolous. One of the signs that this may well be happening to us today is the ubiquity of the word "fun." Notice how much that word is used to describe things that never used to be thought of that way. Recently my niece wrote me that she and her husband were finding their new baby "fun." Someone tours the Metropolitan Museum, comes home and says he had "fun." The next thing you know, people will come home from Mass and tell us that it really was "no fun."

One of the more disturbing aspects of this pan-entertainment culture of ours is the way that category is invading other spheres. For example, we notice that the news is gradually morphing into a form of entertainment. It used to be that the TV news was fairly serious business. Sometimes the ads were a jarring contrast because of their banality or frivolity. But now it is the news itself that is sometimes presented as a form of entertainment. It can also be very disconcerting to be reading a serious magazine and suddenly find yourself in a new genre that is something else altogether. Then you glance at the top of the page and see the notice: "paid political advertisement." When entertainment invades everything, you don't quite know where you are.

Of course, not everything in this world is to be taken seriously. For example, sports have a way of turning into a matter of life and death. Some years ago a South American soccer player was shot dead on the street by an irate fan because he allowed a freak goal in the World Cup.

Clearly something has gone wrong there. Periodically sensible athletes, and especially professional ones, have to remind the fans that sports are just entertainment. When a Chicago Cubs fan interfered with a foul ball that may have cost his downtrodden team the pennant he was run out of town. Hard as it is to take, people have to hear the truth that "after all, it's just a game."

One of the more insidious aspects of constant entertainment is the way it serves to shield us from the truth. If entertainment is basically pleasant distraction, the question has to be asked: from what? The old Romans had a clever trick of providing the population with bread and circuses to keep their minds off the grimness of their lives. With people today, at least in the developed world, ordinary life is not so hard to endure, but what may be harder to bear is the distressing condition of too many other people in our world. Notice that the news now hardly ever focuses on Africa. Why? Maybe because it might cause us sleepless nights.

Another depressing development in the field of entertainment is that humor is no longer very funny. Obviously humor is a matter of taste, but I am not the only one who has noticed that comedy shows now often seem to lack the magic that is essential to real humor. We all know what it is like to watch boring TV shows that supply their own laugh-tracks in the background. It seems to me that for some reason the entertainment world has gradually lost its creative spark. It could be that I am just getting old and crabby. Maybe I have been reading too much John Climacus. But for the life of me I do not find the entertainment industry very entertaining any more.

Hollywood is a perfect example of what has gone wrong. Because film-making involves such vast amounts of money, the choice of subjects cannot be left to the artists and directors. Rather, the bankers and pollsters demand films that will draw people to the box-office. In practical terms that seems to mean simplistic plots spiced up with lots of sex and violence, and so we rarely find a major film any more that actually stretches our capacity to think and feel. People nowadays do not expect to experience serious art in the movie theatre. They go there for distraction. But rather than continue this jeremiad, let me point out some passages in the Rule of Benedict that may speak to this situation.

Laughter and Tears in RB

As our principal text let us read from RB 49, the chapter on Lent. Since monasticism is inherently ascetic, and since Lent is the Great Church's time of ascesis, we might expect that St. Benedict's little treatise will be super-ascetic. That is, in fact, the way it begins: "At all times the lifestyle of a monk ought to have a Lenten quality" (RB 49.1). But after invoking this towering ideal, Benedict comes down to earth: "However, because few have that kind of strength, we urge them to guard their lives with all purity during these Lenten days" (RB 49.2). Then he continues: "The proper way to do this is to restrain ourselves from all evil habits and to devote ourselves to tearful prayer, reading, compunction of heart and asceticism" (RB 49.4).

Nowadays this might strike us as fairly daunting, but it probably did not look that way to Benedict's readers in the sixth century. In fact, the sources for this last verse show that it was standard Lenten thinking for the whole church at that time. In chapter 49 Benedict is not drawing from his usual monastic fonts but instead from the Lenten sermons of Pope Leo the Great. Leo did not preach these sermons to monks but to the people of Rome. So in this chapter we are not looking at super-asceticism but ordinary Christian catechesis, at least in ancient times.

In the text quoted above the thing that caught my notice was the phrase "tearful prayer." What on earth is he talking about? Is that a misprint? As a matter of fact, Benedict uses this same phrase three other times in his Rule (RB 4.55-57; 20.3-4; 52.4), so we can say that it was part of his basic mental horizon. If we do a bit of digging into the early monastic texts, as Irenée Hausherr did in his classic book *Penthos*, we find that the old monks *loved* to weep at prayer. Unlike us, who seem to think them shameful, they thought tears are a gift of God, not something to be avoided but something to savor.

What does that say about people in the sixth century? Could it just mean that they were simple people whose emotions were much closer to the surface than ours? In his book *The Waning of the Middle Ages*, Johannes Huizinga says that medieval people could be made to cry and laugh much more readily than we. A missionary I once talked to in the Philippines said of his aboriginal congregation back in the hills: "They just want me to make them laugh and make them cry." He wasn't being dismissive, just realistic.

Still, there is more going on here in the Rule, for we note the presence of a very significant phrase standing alongside "prayer with tears." Benedict also speaks of "compunction of heart." We probably have a general idea of what that means, but a closer look at the etymology of "compunction" is quite revealing. It refers to the very concrete action of poking something with a sharp object, and even penetrating it. This sounds painful, since the object of this poking is the "heart." But not just any heart; this is a hard heart that needs to be jabbed out of its obtuseness.

Compunction can be achieved in different ways. In Chaim Potok's novel *My Name is Asher Lev*, the Rev, who is a Jewish rabbi, regularly wakes his young son up in the middle of the night. Then he tells him sad and terrible stories to make him weep. What is the point of this apparently sadistic behavior? "I know my son has a mind," says the Rev. "But I want to make sure he also has a soul." In other words, if he can't teach him empathy the game is lost, and tears are a sign of empathy.

But probably Benedict is not thinking of empathy in his chapter on Lent. When he talks about the need for the monk to jab his heart during his Lenten prayer he is surely talking about his conscience. And certainly he wants us to confront our sins during this time. For Benedict is convinced that his monks are sinners. He begins his Rule with a blunt demand that they renounce their sins but he knows they still remain sinners in need of forgiveness and redemption. It was not unknown in past times to run into monks who said they came to the monastery to atone for their sins, and whose monastic existence remained focused on that project. One of our brothers used to make the Stations of the Cross every day of the year, including Christmas.

Before we become completely absorbed in the business of repentance we should notice that Benedict's Lenten program is not entirely mournful. In another verse where he recommends some more Lenten practices, this is what we find: "Let him deny his body some food, some drink, some sleep, some chatter, some joking, and let him await Holy Easter with the joy of spiritual desire." This can hardly be described as a gloomy remark! We see the typical Lenten abstinence from some food and some drink, but what about the rest of it?

To say that his monks should cut back on "some chatter, some joking" implies that they were known to do some of both! That is not the kind of thing you find spelled out in many of the old monastic Rules, nor do you find it in our modern vocation brochures. But it is simply a fact that monks often can be playful. Admittedly, the word used here for "joking" is *scurrilitas*, which in English (as "scurrility") implies dirty or off-color talk. And in fact a lot of the ancient Roman and Greek comedy on stage was extremely foul-mouthed. But the benign meaning of *scurrilitas* is simply "joke."

Benedict has a certain reputation as a sourpuss because at several places in the Rule he warns the monks against laughter. (*risus, scurrilitas*, 4.54; 6.8; 7.59, 60; 43.2; 49.7). I would contend, however, that most of these texts need to be carefully qualified for various reasons. For example, in the Instruments of Good Works it is not just any laughter that is prohibited, but raucous, explosive guffawing. You do hear some of that in the monastery but I think people recognize that not all of it is very mirthful. Sometimes people are just braying out of insecurity, unhappiness, or whatever. A couple of these passages against laughter (especially RB 6.8 and 7.59, 60) are drawn directly from the Rule of the Master, and he really was a humorless character.

At this point, however, we really cannot remain with the ancient mentality. We also need to listen to modern psychology, which usually contends that a sense of humor, far from being an aberration, is quite necessary for a healthy emotional life. That is the case because life is usually long and hard. If we can't see the inherent silliness in much of it and look at it with fond indulgence, then we are in trouble. This is all the more necessary in monastic community life, especially in a small community. There we live so close to one another, really cheek by jowl, that we get to know each other's slightest foibles. If we can't laugh at them we are lost.

As one of my now-deceased confrères used to say, "The best jokes in this place are walking around." This was doubly funny because he was one of the wildest characters in the community, a man whose eccentricities have provided posterity with an endless supply of mirth. He once drove down the freeway the wrong way; when he noticed his error, he backed up—into a big sign that caved in the back of the car. This he did not notice, although he admitted that the "ash fell off my cigar." When he got home he saw the crushed trunk, so he quickly wrote an elaborate explanation, marched into the abbot's office, and flung it down on the desk. The abbot was without a clue, but he knew better than to push the matter with Father Tom.

Rather than descend into anecdotes we should return to the text of RB 49. Certainly Benedict has more to say than just that we should cut back on our silliness during Lent. In fact, he weighs in with one of the most profound remarks in the entire Rule: "Let him await Holy Easter with the joy of spiritual desire" (RB 49.7). If I had to pick out one of Benedict's pithy sayings to take along to a desert island, I think this is one I could not do without, for it is almost breathtaking in its theological vision and also its psychological wisdom.

First we should note the term joy or *gaudium* in Latin. Since we throw this word around fairly casually, it may not strike us as remarkable. Yet it only occurs twice in the entire Rule of Benedict, and both of those usages are found in this same chapter on Lent! Of course this could be interpreted in more than one way. We could say it just proves that Benedict was a really a dour spirit. But that is not at all the case, for there are other signals throughout the Rule that indicate he was anything but glum.

Indeed, one of the most significant pointers to Benedict's essential happiness is his determination that "sadness" (*tristitia*) not pervade his monastery. No less than ten times he goes out of his way to prohibit behavior he fears will bring sadness to the brothers. Life on earth has its inevitable sorrows, some we bring on ourselves and others that cannot be avoided. But where we *can* avoid saddening one another, Benedict demands that we do so. And frankly, it is not easy to maintain good morale in the monastery.

At this point we might refer back to our initial remarks about the Entertainment Culture. Surely the deepest dynamic of that culture is the felt need to promote good morale in society. It is thought that if people can be kept amused at least they won't do anything wicked or harmful to others. Apparently, though, this strategy is not working in the Arab countries, where some people are not at all amused by American pop culture. Even in the monastery monks may try to cope with sadness or depression by immersing themselves in pop culture. But it won't work. And besides, the whole monastic tradition militates against that sort of thing. No, monks need more substantial reasons to be joyful and not sad.

Benedict provides precisely that kind of solid reason for Lenten joy, for he insists that it is based on longing for Holy Easter. In fact, he uses an especially pungent expression for this longing: "the joy of spiritual desire" (*spiritalis desiderii gaudio*). Someone with a delicate sense of human foibles might question Benedict's use of "desire" in this sentence. After all, isn't Lent precisely about the suppression of our desires? No doubt that has some truth to it, but it might also be that we have an excessively ethereal idea of the spiritual life. Could it not be possible that Lent is about *increasing* our longing or desire? Remember that the longing is for Holy Easter, not for carnal things.

"Spiritual joy" can be a key to understanding the word "desire" in this sentence. "Spiritual" in this verse could refer directly to the Holy Spirit. So Benedict is talking here about a gift of the Holy Spirit and not just some virtue we exercise by sheer will. At any rate, the "joy" he is discussing here is a special kind of joy. It is by no means superficial happiness that can evaporate at the slightest setback. This is a deep joy that can even coexist with serious human suffering. I can be joyful when I am dying of cancer.

But the deepest dimension of this whole notion of spiritual longing is the goal, namely, Holy Easter. We must remember that Lent is not self-contained; it is not meant for itself. No, it is strictly a run-up to Easter. No matter how seriously Christians take their Lenten asceticism, it is not really the point. It is not the bottom line. All this Lenten seriousness culminates in the resurrection of Jesus Christ from the dead, and also in the promise that if we are with him in his carrying of the cross we will also be with him in our own resurrection. Since this is the whole goal of our Lent, it ought not to be a grim or depressing exercise.

Notice, please, that Benedict does not say that we may be sorrowful now but with Easter we will be joyful. Jesus says something like that (the woman in childbirth), but at least in RB 49 Benedict teaches that Lent itself ought to be joyful. Since we know very well what it is leading up to, our Lent should be suffused with deep joy. If we are in Christ we have no reason at all to be dejected or despondent. Psychologically we may still struggle with these tendencies, but theologically we are already "citizens of heaven," with no reason to lack joy.

Chapter Two

Monastic Recreation

When I first came to monastic life in the 1950s one of the official exercises was what was called "recreation." It consisted of a period after supper, but sometimes also after lunch, when the group gathered in a room set aside for relaxation. The monks did various things during this gathering, such as play cards, converse, read the newspapers, or perhaps play billiards. The key thing was that they did it *together* and it was a set part of the horarium. Normally you did not absent yourself from recreation.

Rule of Benedict

Given its official status, it is legitimate to ask what St. Benedict has to say about monastic recreation. The answer is monosyllabic: nothing. If you inspect RB 48, which sets out the daily horarium of the monks in a fairly detailed fashion, there is no mention of recreation. In fact, it is almost impossible to find a few minutes in that schedule where the community could participate in what we now call recreation. RB 48 seems quite determined to fill out the day with three essential monastic activities: prayer, *lectio divina*, and work. Obviously there had to be time for meals and for sleep, but other than that it is a rather tight program.

Yet it is not quite as tight as what the Master devises in RM 50. In that longer chapter, on which RB 48 is apparently based, the earlier author displays an almost puritanical attitude toward the use of time by the monks. He says plainly that if the monks have any free time they are sure to commit sin (RM 50.1-4). Therefore he is determined to keep them busy every moment! Benedict seems to back off from this kind of hysterical fear of leisure. He merely says: "Idleness is the enemy of the soul," which should not be expanded into anything resembling the Master's neurosis. In the old days our hard-working Germanic monastic monks in America sometimes displayed a similar allergy to leisure.

If we think of recreation as communication between persons it might seem to violate Benedict's sixth chapter. That rather hard-edged condensation of a long, rambling discussion in the RM concerning who could dare to ask the abbot a question (RM 8–9) is summarized by Benedict into a forbidding program of silence. The author is not just referring to sins of the tongue, which he also inveighs against in Prologue 26-27. No, he seems to be ruling out *all* conversation between the members of the community. Can he possibly be serious about this? How could his monks get along without talking? It seems they did not, as we can gather from his offhand remarks in other parts of the Rule.

For example, in RB 43.8 Benedict discusses the problem of monks who come late to the Divine Office. In general he hates tardiness, but he hesitates to bar the doors on such people as they sometimes do in modern theatres. No, he wants them to come into the choir and take up a place reserved for latecomers. If they stay outside, he says, "There may be those who would return to bed and sleep, or, worse yet, settle down outside and engage in idle talk, thereby giving occasion to the Evil One" (Eph 4:27). For our purposes here I think the interesting aspect of this passage is not what it says but what it implies. Benedict is not dealing with mere hypothetical possibilities: he knew his monks liked to gossip, and there must have been plenty of that going on for him to try to cut it down.

The same conclusion seems warranted in regard to RB 49.7 concerning the program he proposes for the community during Lent. "Let each one deny himself some food, drink, sleep, needless talking and idle jesting, and look forward to holy Easter with joy and spiritual longing." Of course abstinence from food, drink, and sleep was standard Lenten procedure for all Christians, and not just monks, in former years. The theological heart of the verse lies in the idea of Lent as joyful preparation for "holy Easter." But what fascinates me is Benedict's serene suggestion that the monks cut back on their "needless talking and idle jesting" during Lent: not cut it out altogether, just "deny themselves *some*" frivolity. It certainly does not suggest that his monastery was a grim sort of morgue where no one dared to tell a joke.

One more foray into the Rule should suffice to make our point. In RB 48, discussing *lectio divina*, Benedict lays down the following provision: "Above all, one or two seniors must surely be deputed to make the rounds of the monastery while the brothers are reading. Their duty is to see that no brother is so apathetic as to waste time or engage in idle talk to the neglect of his reading, and so not only harm himself but also distract others" (RB 48.17-18).

Here again I don't believe the author is merely spinning unlikely and unfortunate possibilities. He certainly knows all about gabby and restless monks who find *lectio divina* a difficult exercise because it requires sitting still and keeping quiet. Elsewhere he says that such people are to be given some work to do, even on Sunday. Otherwise they can constitute a menace in the community for other people who *do* want peace and quiet for reading and meditation.

In our own time we hear a lot about ADS, attention disorder syndrome, in persons whose chemical makeup prevents them from concentrating for any extended period of time. We also know that television programming has the tendency to encourage hyperactivity in those who watch it a lot. In other words, we live in a jumpy age. But are we really so different from Benedict's own monks? He too was dealing with restless, chatty, and sometimes even feckless people who apparently needed to talk to each other.

Recreation as a Basic Human Need

From the beginning of this chapter we have been looking at recreation not as some kind of unfortunate exception to a serious, disciplined monastic life. Rather, we have been operating on the assumption that it is positively necessary. If we look at recreation purely in terms of relaxation we might recall the story of Antony, the great iconic hermit of the Egyptian desert. The story is worth quoting verbatim:

> A hunter in the desert saw Abba Antony enjoying himself with the brethren and he was shocked. Wanting to show him that it was necessary sometimes to meet the needs of the brethren, the old man said to him: "Put an arrow in your bow and shoot it." So he did. The old man then said, "Shoot another," and he did so. Then the old man said "Shoot yet again," and the hunter replied "If I bend my bow so much I will break it." Then the old man said to him, "It is the same with the work of God. If we stretch the brethren beyond measure they will soon break. (*Sayings of the Desert Fathers*, Antony 3)

It is good that we have this story about a Desert Father, for otherwise we might get the idea that the early monks lived in perpetual silence and seriousness. In fact, there is plenty of evidence to indicate that they loved to visit each other in their cells, which usually were not too far distant from one another. No doubt they did this for various purposes, important among them being spiritual direction and conversation about the things of God. The *Conferences* of John Cassian are a prime example of this latter activity. Whether or not Cassian is recording verbatim conversations, it is clear that he thinks it is important for people to talk to each other about what they hold dear to their hearts.

Although it is probably not helpful to define recreation too narrowly as conversation, that is the side of it I want to emphasize in this chapter. I have no wish to downplay the therapeutic value of things like hobbies that are often pursued alone. Indeed, many wholesome hobbies have immense value for those involved since they are, so to speak, transported to a separate world where they can forget the problems and tensions of their lives. Anybody who has gotten deeply involved in stamp collecting, crosswords, knitting, and so on knows how much this can contribute to mental health. But that is not my subject here. I want to say that some kind of communication is absolutely essential to human happiness. Where this is thwarted or even entirely lacking, there will be trouble.

Actually, we have a historical example of how this impacted monks. The Trappists are the religious Order famous for silence. Indeed, before Vatican II their system of hand signs in place of verbal speech was well known throughout the Catholic Church. But hand signs can only go so far in replacing conversation, for there are many things that can only be expressed in language. Many Trappists will now admit that their hand signs were far from adequate, and that whenever they got the chance—say, on a car trip—they frantically pumped each other for information. About what? About who they were! The problem was that they had little or no idea of the background of their next-door neighbor in the monastery, and that was experienced as an inhuman hardship.

In fact, complete silence was not the authentic tradition of the Cistercian Order, but a seventeenth-century invention by the great reformer Abbot De Rancé. How do we know this? One example from my own experience may serve to illustrate. When I visited the idyllic ruins of Fountains Abbey in northern England, I remember noticing scratched on the stone floor of the former infirmary what was obviously a board game, perhaps something like checkers. Could it be possible that the twelfth-century Cistercians actually played games in the infirmary? Yes, indeed, it is. For them the infirmary was often a sort of vacation place where they would go to be bled. But when they were there they were allowed a relaxed schedule, including plenty of time for rest and leisurely conversation. This is a very attractive picture, at least to me.

Another incident that comes to mind regarding recreation as a basic human need concerns a visit I made to the famous Italian abbey of Camaldoli. This place is high up in the Apennines, but perched on the side of a deep ravine. The hermitages are even higher up on the mountain but in a more open setting. At any rate, I was somewhat apprehensive about my visit since this community had a reputation for considerable austerity. Wasn't I surprised when I found them anything but taciturn! In fact, they seemed to converse almost everywhere—in "dialogue homilies," at table, in the corridors. I was intrigued by this behavior, so I asked the abbot, who happened to be a former teacher of mine in Rome.

He said that it was important to notice the location of the monastery. It is so deep in the ravine that the sun hardly gets down there in the winter, never mind that the Italian winters are often very cloudy. He said that all that gloom and darkness have a saddening effect on his confrères, even plunging some of them into psychosomatic illness. As abbot he felt he needed to try to remedy this situation; he was also tired of the big medical bills. So he decided to let the monks communicate freely. He claimed it was doing wonders for them. To me this looked like a good application of the maxim of pop psychology: communicate or die!

Even that most ascetic of all Orders, the Carthusians, does not entirely eschew recreation. Once a week the whole group goes for a hike in the countryside around the monastery. In the film *Into the Great Silence*, which is a stunning documentary filmed in the Grande Chartreuse high up in the French Alps, the weekly hike appears to be a truly humane occasion. Rather than being on any kind of stoical forced march, the small group is shown resting on a patio and casually chatting about the week's events. One of the monks is flying out to Korea the next morning, so that is a topic of discussion.

What makes this seemingly ordinary conversation so poignant is that the rest of the film is marked by the most profound *silence*. This is a truly quiet monastery, where people rarely say a word. Indeed, the silence at the Grande Chartreuse is so palpable that it is said that some viewers in American movie theatres have fled in terror a few minutes into this three-hour film. The recording equipment used to make this film is so acute that even very slight sounds that normally hardly register on our ear stand out loud and clear. Nevertheless, even these giants of solitude and silence gather once a week to communicate with each other.

Recreation in Different Settings and Cultures

Rather than theorizing about recreation it is probably better to experience it first hand. When one does that in various settings in different cultures, the results are interesting. It should come as no surprise that people in different cultures would need to find their own style of relaxation and mutual sharing. Of course, it is hard to know much about the recreation of a given community unless you spend more than a few days there, but here are some typical recreation periods I have observed in various countries.

French monasticism is famously austere. For example, although French food in general is exquisite I have always found the food in the French monasteries nearly inedible. So I expected that their recreation would have some of that same harshness about it. At Fleury (St. Benoît sur Loire), things did not seem very promising. At first recreation seemed almost like a chapter meeting, with the abbot holding forth in the front and the monks all turned toward him as an audience. He proceeded to discuss various items that had come in the mail that day while making comments about recent happenings. It all seemed incredibly patriarchal, and I remember musing that my own confrères would never put up with anything like that.

But at some point the abbot invited other monks to comment on things. I presume it had to do with their various departments and activities. (My spoken French is nonexistent.) Whatever they were talking about, pretty soon they were all talking. What started out as a highly formal, one-dimensional exercise in abbatial authority turned into a very lively communal discussion. It was a lesson to me not to make snap judgments. Every group has its own way of communicating. The exact form in which they do so is less important than the fact that they do so.

Another recreation that began rather inauspiciously took place in England. The first time I was invited into recreation at Downside Abbey, I noticed that the chairs were arranged in a very distinctive and almost frightening pattern. Each of these straight-backed seats was part of a perfect circle in which one had no choice but to sit next to someone and talk to them. The spatial rigidity was somewhat softened by the fact that each man got himself a cup of coffee or tea on a saucer, which he then balanced in his hand. When seated, people did not talk at random, but only to the partner on one side. The whole thing was very English: quiet and sedate. But it was also obvious that people were actually communicating.

This particular community also taught me a lesson in perception. I had been there once before, as an unknown monastic guest, and I had found them rather frosty. At least there was little attempt to reach out to me. When they invited me to give their retreat many years later I was rather apprehensive. Would they even acknowledge my presence? In fact, almost every single monk came to my room to visit with me, go to confession, just communicate. Far from being cold, they were one of the warmest communities I ever encountered. But they did it in their own way. No loud backslapping. No boisterous large groups. Just one-to-one conversation of a highly personal nature.

The Italians are usually not so formal. Once I was staying at the Abbey of San Giorgio in Venice, which has to be one of the world's most picturesque monastic settings. The place is on a tiny island right across from San Marco and the Palace of the Doges. One evening I was reading in my room and I glanced out the open window. Lo and behold, between me and San Marco was a brightly lit cruise ship silently making its way through the lagoon. Meanwhile, down in church one of the monks was playing the flute while accompanying himself on the organ pedals. Shades of Vivaldi!

At any rate, after dinner the monks said the customary after-meal prayers but then sat back down to open their mail and engage in a fairly boisterous, free-flowing discussion. This rather unusual form of monastic recreation must have been the norm, since it lasted until vespers. It seemed a natural extension of the meal, which is something Italians are very good at. Go into any neighborhood *trattoria* for supper and you will find families and friends lingering over long, leisurely meals. They are in absolutely no hurry to finish up and get home. If you are yourself in a hurry you may have considerable difficulty finding the waiter to make out your bill.

It seems that the recreation at San Giorgio was satisfying to more than the monks. They said one of their regular visitors had been the Patriarch of Venice, Angelo Roncalli, a.k.a. John XXIII. He used to get lonely eating alone in his palace across the water, so he would hop on the *vaporetto* (motor taxi) and come over to join the monks at table. He would then plop down, light up a cigarette, and proceed to gab and tell jokes. They said he loved to talk, so much so that during siesta time he did not nap but sat by his open window on the ground floor of the patriarchal residence chatting with passersby. He should have been a cenobite.

Contemporary Problems with Recreation

At the end of a recent visitation in our community I asked the visitators to comment on our recreation, which I find somewhat lacking. They retorted that they found it considerably better than what goes on in their own communities! Of course, it may have been that while they were with us our recreation *was* fairly impressive. Maybe more people showed up, and maybe they actually communicated. Still, their report about their own houses was depressing. Could it be that recreation has become a problem in most of our houses? I think that is the case, but I am not sure most monks are looking for a solution.

The fact is that some monasteries have extremely low expectations for recreation. One monastery I visited lately has one half-hour recreation period once a week. When one sees the recreation room one ceases to wonder why people do not want to go there. It is dark and quite forbidding, with nothing but hard, straight-backed furniture. None of the chairs were arranged in such a way as to facilitate conversation. Instead, it seems that someone wished to *prevent* communication. I indicated above that you can have a perfectly good conversation on hard furniture, but it certainly doesn't invite people to linger. Certainly no one is going to accuse that community of fostering a family atmosphere in that kind of room.

Yet if you listen to some monks in this country, you might think that recreation is more or less beside the point. Recently a good friend of mine, a member of a famous old monastery, insisted to me that his community has *no recreation*. When I pressed him on this apparently heretical statement he stood his ground. "But, I said, you have a beautiful recreation room. Surely something must happen there?" "No, he said, there is no recreation period and there is no recreation!" It was almost as if he were determined to keep a family disgrace buried and out of sight. He was not apologetic, nor did he act as if it was a problem area for them.

The opposite reaction occurred once when I was visiting a different but equally large and famous monastery. One day I asked one of the monks about so and so, who was an old acquaintance of mine. Since I had not seen him in three or four days I wondered if he was on vacation or perhaps ill. "No," he said, "he is home. But he never comes to recreation." I was willing to let it go at that, but my interlocutor was not. He said quite loudly and deliberately: "No one is a monk of X unless he comes to recreation!" I think that was one of the most arresting statements I had heard in a long time. I did not ask him to exegete it, but I thought about it a lot. After a little more inquiry I determined that my old friend was indeed a rather marginal member of this community who rarely appeared at public functions. He was a good teacher, but not much of a cenobitic monk.

Is there such a thing as too much recreation? Of course there is. There can be too much of anything. One abbey I know lives by a schedule that is truly bizarre, at least to my way of thinking. They have vespers soon after supper. Then there is recreation after vespers—until bedtime! Since vespers is over by 7:30, that means that recreation can theoretically extend till at least 10 p.m. In fact, some monks play cards well into the night. They have been doing this for years and, God bless them, they seem to love it. But it is in flagrant violation of the Holy Rule of St. Benedict. Even though recreation has to have an element of freedom about it, it also has to be subject to discipline.

It could be said, I suppose, that there is something intrinsically absurd about demanding that people come to recreation. If recreation is by definition a form of enjoyment, then what sense does it make to treat it as compulsory? In the old days it certainly was compulsory, at least for monks in formation. I do not know whether all the senior monks attended recreation, but surely most of them did. Nowadays, however, it appears that most communities hesitate to treat recreation as mandatory. Even novices do not seem to be required to attend. How can they be so required when the novice master does not attend? Recreation has ceased to be an official community exercise.

Probably most of us have heard about communities of nuns where in the past recreation consisted of the whole group getting together to shell peas. We used to chuckle over this because it seemed so contrary to what we consider recreation. Yet was it so misguided? In our community we have recently begun the practice of folding and stuffing our periodic begging letters during recreation. Everybody is expected to come to this "party," and the monks do come. Furthermore, they seem to enjoy it. Somehow this mindless handwork seems to facilitate at least casual conversation and people rarely complain about it. So it could be that some of the old forms were in fact more effective than we think in facilitating community life.

When we try to analyze the causes of our decreasing taste for common recreation, there is no doubt that individualism is a huge factor. If I see it as primarily a time to enjoy myself I may not be willing to engage in something that is less than satisfying. The whole idea of *contributing* to a group activity for the sake of the group and not myself seems rather alien to our culture, at least when it comes to recreation. People who are very hard workers, and who would never think of missing a work assignment, now presume permission to miss recreation and do miss it regularly.

If they are not there, what are they doing? Probably they are engrossed in some computer activity or watching TV. These electronic devices have made deep inroads into our monasteries. They are probably not completely individualistic in usage, but let's be honest, not many people deal with the Internet in any but single fashion. You can watch television as a group and do some sharing, but usually it is just one individual with the TV. Too often these devices are an alternative to dealing with another living, breathing human being. That is what recreation is about: trying to relate to my brother, rain or shine, no matter how I feel or how he feels. We come together and maybe we just sit. But we are together.

Chapter Three

Partisan Politics
and the
Benedictine Chapter

Partisan Politics

In beginning this essay I had to consult the dictionary to see whether there is an abstract noun to go with "partisan." I found "partisanship," but it is so unusual that I decided to do without it. Even the word "partisan" isn't used much any more, but that does not mean that the reality has disappeared from our midst. Indeed, our society is currently consumed by partisan emotions to such an extent that shouting is replacing reasoned argument and the very idea of calm objectivity is little respected. To put all this in perspective, let us think a bit about democracy itself. Since I am no political scientist this will have to be a vague sketch, based on impressions.

Democracy means the rule of the *demos* or people, and in the case of the United States it has come to mean a two-party system in which power is contested in regular elections. Other countries have parliamentary democracies while we have a republican form, but it comes down to much the same thing. The crucial thing is that power is not the monopoly of one party, as was the case in Mexico for most of the twentieth century. When we hear of a "democracy" where the ruling party garners 99 percent of the vote we smell a rat.

In a system such as ours we have majority rule by one means or another. Because of our arcane rules it is sometimes possible for the person with fewer votes to become president, but that is an anomaly that does not bring down the system. At any rate, where you have majority rule it is necessary to think about the rights and sensibilities of the minority. It makes no sense to trample on them for four years if we expect their loyalty. As for the minority, they need to understand that their position is not a subversive one. They should be a loyal minority, not an enemy of the state.

After over two hundred years of democratic government in our country we can say that it has served us very well. Sometimes we find it a maddeningly slow way to come to consensus, but by and large it works. We have had only one violent revolution in two hundred years; we have had only one president resign; we have had regular alternation between the parties. All of this is somewhat miraculous, given the fact that people regularly immigrate into this country from very different political backgrounds. Not all of them get the point right away, but so far our system has not collapsed of its own weight and complexity.

Still, we have to have some sense of history about all this. Our system was actually designed by a group of men who had a very different social vision than most of us do today. The simple fact that almost all the signers of the Declaration of Independence were Masons ought to tell us something. Furthermore, most of them were Deists who did not believe in the divinity of Jesus Christ, a fact that might cause some of our Fundamentalists a bit of heartburn. We should also remember that our founders were men of the Enlightenment, with elitist views that favored rich white males over everybody else. But by and large they cobbled together a brilliant system.

One of the aspects of our political system I have been thinking about lately is the relationship of democracy to capitalism. The very fact that the original arrangement only allowed property owners to vote indicates that these two things were very closely aligned in their minds. Nowadays that seems like a quaint idea, but for them it was a matter of course. What concerns me, however, is the question of whether the principles of capitalism have not unduly influenced, I almost said "infected," democracy. The capitalist tenet that is most worrisome is the one that teaches us to take care of Number One.

I have heard that Adam Smith did not blatantly teach that self-interest was the attitude that makes capitalism run. Still, it does not seem to embarrass his followers in our own time to claim that this principle is what makes our economy work. In recent times we had the version of this called "trickle-down economics," which suggests that when the rich are allowed to pursue their self-interest to the maximum there will still be a benevolent side effect of economic prosperity percolating down to the poor. As far as I know there is no proof at all that this is the way things actually work. All I know is that the last thirty or so years have seen the rich in this country become ultra-rich.

In itself that is not intrinsically evil, but social historians point out that one of the most important requirements in a democracy is that the gap between the rich and the poor not become too wide. It has become a yawning chasm in this country, which scares the bejeebers out of thoughtful people. But rather than wander off into a discussion of economics, where I am profoundly ignorant, let me return to an area where I am only partially benighted, namely, politics.

We seem to have arrived at a state of widespread political vindictiveness in this country. First of all, there are the endless presidential campaigns with the strange spectacle of bitter warfare without much substance. Things are now fought out on television, which costs barrels of money to use if you want to buy campaign ads. Recently the Supreme Court has taken the astonishing step of ruling that there can be no limit to what corporations can spend on political campaigns. In effect this means that they can control television if they wish. This was decided on the grounds that corporations are "moral persons" with complete individual personal rights. Never mind that giant corporations are a very serious political problem because they are international and not under national control. The court has decided that we need no protection from these shadowy entities.

At any rate, we have come a long, long way in the history of political campaigns. Before, say, 1930 the campaigns were much shorter. Some candidates did not even bother to move around making speeches; they sat at home and let other people speak for them. The whole thing was more civil and casual than it is now. When Benjamin Harrison's wife died a couple of weeks before the election in 1892 he simply stayed home and grieved. He lost, but it probably wasn't because he didn't campaign. I say that because his opponent, Grover Cleveland, also did not campaign out of a sense of sympathy.

What is political vindictiveness? It is the attitude that if we don't win at least we can bring down the other party, make it hard or impossible for them to govern. When Bill Clinton charmed his way into the White House in 1992, Trent Lott said that the Republican Congress would give him a couple months of happiness before they brought him down. And that is pretty much what happened. They dug up enough dirt to keep Bill on the defensive for eight years. Of course, Bill was his own worst enemy. He didn't need other people to hobble his administration; he did enough dumb things to damage it himself.

To my mind the disturbing, even shocking thing here is the very idea that the opposition party's program is to *destroy* the ruling executive. My question is: Who, then, is supposed to run the country? Or doesn't it really matter who runs the country? This last question seems absurd, but it is not, because the sad fact is that a certain number of people and their leaders have decided that this country does not need to be run at all. A significant group has developed such a negative attitude toward government itself that their basic mission is to either shut down the government or render it virtually impotent. So we now have the remarkable phenomenon of people being elected to Congress on the platform of shutting down the government.

Of course, the political process in Congress is set up to prevent any party from running roughshod over the minority. Important legislation usually takes a long time to work through the system. The minority possesses certain tools such as the filibuster and other tactics that can slow things down. This can be a problem when Congress must act quickly or not at all. But when you throw in the added factor of legislators who want to block *all* legislation you have the recipe for political gridlock.

And what about the straight party vote, a thing that happens over and over? Perhaps it is sometimes inevitable, since the parties do have certain basic principles such as states' rights for the Republicans and minority rights for the Democrats. But many of the issues that are debated and fought over in Congress are so complex and nuanced that one wonders how the votes could be so clear-cut? Could it be that the whole thing has become so partisan that it does not really matter much what is at stake—if the other guys are for it, we are against it? How does this really differ from a playground brawl or gang warfare? What has this got to do with rational decision-making?

Then there is the question of representation. What is the obligation of a senator or congressman to his or her constituency? Is her job simply to promote the interests of her constituents in the legislative process? That seems to be the attitude many people in this country have toward their congressional delegation. The key question is: "What has he brought home for us lately?" rather than "What has he done for the common good?" That last phrase should not go unremarked. Indeed, it could be described as the key to this whole discussion: how can we promote the common good? If this question appears odd or even unintelligible to enough voters we have a huge problem. It could be that we have become basically ungovernable.

With little or no appreciation of the common good, political life just devolves into self-interest. Since that is the basis of capitalism, maybe the question then is whether we are being done in by our capitalism. Actually, we are being done in by a lot of things. If the cultural basis of democracy is an electorate that is able and willing to understand the issues, we are already in deep trouble. How many people now have the stomach to actually study the issues? That means reading, not just reacting to a pretty face on TV. There is evidence of shocking political ignorance in this country.

A disturbing aspect of our political naïveté is our distaste for straight talk from our politicians. Sad to say, most politicians no longer dare to discuss issues with their constituents; they provide them with comforting nostrums or, worse yet, they play to their lowest instincts. Of course, some of this concerns the very nature of democratic politics: you have to get elected. And if you want to stay in the legislature you have to get reelected. To do this you have to keep people happy. But what if people really need to hear some hard truths? Those truths may be essential to their long-term happiness but hard on their short-term blood pressure.

Just one example before I exit politics. I live in a state that is one of the premiere energy producers in the country. We have it all: coal, oil, wind, you name it. It is in our short-term interest to exploit our coal and oil to the maximum. But in the interest of the whole planet it behooves us to conserve our resources, or at least not to misuse them. We are, after all, citizens of planet earth. Even though coal burning is one of the worst of all environmental problems, no politician can get elected in North Dakota by facing up to this issue. So we are talked to like children. Maybe we are all complicit in living with lies for our short-term interest. Let us exit the sordid realm of politics for the pure, unpolluted heights of the Rule of St. Benedict.

The Benedictine Chapter Meeting

Before we try to talk about the monastic chapter meeting as it is presented to us in RB 3 we have to recall the basic polity of the Benedictine monastery. For our purpose here, which is to compare it to American politics, we have to note right away that the Benedictine system is not democratic. It is heavily based on the rule of an abbot or similar superior, which makes it decidedly hierarchic. This hierarchic character can be emphasized or deemphasized, depending on the ambient culture, but it cannot be entirely swept away if one is to remain within the polity of the Benedictine Rule.

Having said that, I find myself immediately searching for a way to keep all this separate from the general polity of the Catholic Church. We often hear it said, especially by the Vatican, that the church is not a democracy. In that sense, at least, the Benedictine community is like the church; it is not a democracy. But one might then be excused the important followup question: if the church is not a democracy, then what is it? Well, nobody wants to say it is a monarchy because monarchs are no longer fashionable in our world. There is not one absolute monarch left standing in Europe.

For much of its history the Catholic Church has operated much like an absolute monarchy, with the pope supreme on the world scale and the bishop supreme on the local level. There is nothing in the New Testament to make such a system mandatory for the church of Jesus Christ. On the other hand, it *is* true that very early in church history you have writers like Ignatius of Antioch (110 AD) who talk as if the monarchical bishop is the logical form Christian leadership should take.

Getting back to the Benedictine polity, after we have established that the abbot is very important in the Rule we should add that he is not *all*-important. For example, there is a crucial text in RB 1.2 that says about the cenobites that they "live in monasteries and serve under a rule and an abbot." That terse statement needs some unpacking. Notice, first of all, that the abbot is only one element of three that figure in the life of the cenobite. Indeed, if we are to take the series order seriously he is the third factor for the monk, not the first. First comes the monastery, that is, the community; next comes the Rule; then comes the abbot.

In the existential order this same structure proves to be true. How does an abbot get made? He is elected by the monks, from their ranks. That means that the community comes first, then the abbot. Without a community you have no abbot. No matter how many megalomaniacs claim to be abbots looking for monks to follow them, they are deluding themselves. Abbots do not make monasteries; monasteries make abbots. This is even more apparent in some of the pre-Benedictine cenobitic Rules. For example, neither Basil nor Augustine even gets around to *mentioning* the superior until late in their Rules. The Rule of the Master, which Benedict followed closely for seven chapters before he got sick of it, does make the abbot supreme. But Benedict saw clearly enough that he had to tone down some of its abbot-centeredness.

Moreover, even though Benedict teaches a pretty daunting level of obedience, he does not make the abbot's will supreme. In fact, RB 2, which puts the abbot on a very high pedestal, alternatively warns him that he is not an autocrat; he answers to God. It is easy enough for an autocrat to ward off disagreeable challenges to his authority by invoking his divine relationship. But Benedict makes it clear enough that the abbot is also answerable to the community for his decisions. Furthermore, the Catholic Church has laid down good, practical procedures for community decisions that include the secret ballot on important questions. So the abbot cannot just do whatever he wants.

RB 2 is still a pretty authoritarian treatise. Yet it appears that Benedict himself eventually found it unbearable! At least he crafted a second treatise on the abbot, namely, RB 64, which is much less harsh in tone. Rather than setting the abbot on the heights and then threatening him with the depths, RB 64 takes a more realistic and pastoral approach to monastic leadership. Drawing heavily on Saint Augustine's writings, Benedict insists that the best way to lead people is to draw them on with the allurement of kindness and consideration, not coercion. So the Rule itself is self-correcting in this regard.

There are, however, parts of the Rule that teach a very rigid and almost draconian form of obedience. For example, RB 5 calls for a kind of instant obedience that people today generally find repulsive and crushing. We do not live in a historical vacuum, and by now we are well aware of what instant, unquestioning obedience can produce. It can yield Auschwitz and Jonestown plus a lot more mischief that is not so famous. Still, when we read the Rule a bit more carefully it becomes apparent that the monks are not children to simply be ordered here and there. Unlike the Rule of the Master, in which no one but the abbot has any discretionary power, Benedict's officials, for example, have to make decisions of their own. He does not seem to want robots around him.

Yet it cannot be denied that the Rule of Benedict leaves the impression that the abbot is the primary agent of decision-making in the monastery. For example, even in a chapter like RB 31, which presents the cellarer as a very important official with all kinds of responsibility, he is warned over and over again not to act outside the parameters set down by the abbot. It is not hard to imagine how superiors used to see this as a mandate to do everything themselves. Many cellarers had no real power at all; they were just functionaries. Some of them were not even allowed to carry keys!

For an example of how far this kind of thinking can go it is enough to dip into RB 33, where it is stated that monks may not have personal possessions "because they have neither their bodies nor their own wills at their own disposal. Rather, they should ask for all they need from the father of the monastery." It would not be hard to blow those two verses up into an absolute nightmare of overweening and abusive authority. Monks nowadays don't like to think about such statements. They know very well that they *do* have wills of their own. They have vowed to consult first the will of God and not their own desires, but one never is relieved of the considerable moral responsibility of choosing what is right.

What we have outlined above is not just a theory. It is put into effect in various ways in the monastic life. One of the ways this plays out it is in the monastic chapter. To put it bluntly, the monastic chapter meeting is not democratic. It may involve the kind of open discussion that characterizes democratic meetings, but the basic structure of the meeting is not democratic. The abbot is completely in charge. He calls the chapter into session, he proposes the question or questions, he listens to the advice he is given, and then he decides what should be done. All of this is very plainly stated in RB 3, the wonderful little chapter on the chapter meeting. And yet it may not be understood very well, even by the monks.

I say this because of the experience we had with our new constitutions in 1989. At that time it was spelled out very clearly that the abbot is not a voter in the monastic chapter. Some of the abbots were not happy about this, complaining that they were being deprived of their monastic voting rights! In fact it was simply a logical working out of what the Rule itself has to say. The basic structure of the chapter is that the abbot asks the monks for advice. If he were to vote he would in effect be giving himself advice. Indeed, one of our abbots adamantly insisted in the Senior Council that not only did he have a vote, he also had the tie-breaker. So he thought he should dominate the whole process.

I should interject here that the Rule has nothing about votes, and especially about secret ballots. But Canon Law gives the monks the right to vote on the admittance of new candidates and also on large expenditures of money. Still, the initiative comes from the abbot: the monks only *allow* the abbot to receive the candidate or spend the money. They themselves never initiate the action. Apparently the church has judged that the Benedictine chapter needs a component of secrecy to protect the right of the monk to express himself on big questions without fear of disclosure. I am all in favor of this, since sometimes abbots need salutary opposition. For example, one of our abbots once introduced a consultative vote by telling the monks that their vote would not affect his decision one way or the other. So naturally the monks used the opportunity to vote a resounding *no*! Then he was furious.

The position of the abbot in the chapter is a delicate one. He is to "arrange things with foresight and justice." He is to ponder what he hears from the brothers and then decide what he thinks is "more useful" (*utilius*) for the community. Now, that sounds pretty bland and even secular, but there is reason to think that *utilis* was a Christian word. At the very least it refers to the common good, which is a very, very important concept. A similar adjective Benedict uses for the abbot's discretionary process is *salubrius*: he is to pursue what seems "most beneficial for salvation." This vocabulary shows that we are not dealing with mere pragmatic judgments here, much less power politics.

In my commentary on this chapter (*Benedict's Rule* [= BR] 78), I indicated that I consider the virtue of discernment particularly crucial to the monastic decision-making process. This virtue is not just about choosing what is right but about sorting out varying opinions about what is right. That is precisely what the abbot has to do in the chapter, at least according to RB 3. It is assumed that there will be different views on things and that these should be expressed. Indeed, Benedict encourages the most timid of the brothers, namely, the youngest, to speak their minds. The abbot must respect these various opinions, no matter who enunciates them. Then he has to choose what he thinks best.

I would like to introduce a bit of comparative criticism to sharpen this point. In the Rule of the Master, regarding the monastic chapter, we find the following curious remark:

> The counsel of all is to be sought because sometimes there are as many diverse opinions as there are people—all at once the best advice may well be given by one from whom it was least expected, and this may redound most to the common good—and from the many opinions the one to choose will be easy to find. (RM 2.44-46)

We can see here some of the same ideas Benedict has incorporated into his chapter 3. But there are also a couple of rather strange comments that do not jibe with Benedict's point of view on the chapter. The Master seems to think that the more opinions the better, which may indeed be the kind of thinking that sometimes results in "brainstorming," for which I can see the value in certain situations. But the Master also gives the impression that all these opinions are just sort of cannon fodder for the abbot's discernment process. From there it is not a big step to basic disrespect for the opinions of others. And the closing comment that "the one to choose will be easy to find" indicates that the Master is not exactly agonizing over the complexity of issues. He knows what he wants.

Pardon me for being hard on the poor old Master, but I have experienced a certain kind of abbatial disregard that is at total variance with RB 3. Sometimes an abbot really does not care all that much what the community thinks or wants in regard to a certain question. He goes through the motions of calling the chapter, posing the question, and listening. But subtle indicators such as body language make it quite clear that the abbot has already made up his mind. He is just putting in time. If this is the case, he himself could be the biggest loser.

For example, my monastery underwent a terrible bankruptcy in 1924 that came very close to ending our history forever. The community was dispersed for four years and the debt was never repaid. The superior who presided over the beginning of this debacle was once asked how he could have let it happen. Why did he not consult his chapter before making these reckless expenditures? His answer was very revealing: "They were all just inexperienced young men new in this country, with no idea of money or practicalities." This was before the Code of Canon Law of 1917, so none of this was illegal. But it was foolish in the extreme, an example of the blind leading the blind. My own gut feeling about such things is this: it is better to be wrong along with others than to be right alone.

Before I go any farther into anecdotal wonderland let me return to RB 3, and especially to the second half of the equation, namely, the role of the monk and the community in the chapter meeting. Actually, Chapter 3 is written as a kind of dialogue between the two roles, authority and response. It is by no means just about the abbot, who is not the only responsible adult in the Rule of Benedict. What is the job of the monk in the chapter meeting? We have already seen that it is to advise the abbot on issues the abbot proposes.

Now, this would seem to be a pretty straightforward idea, but it is remarkable how poorly it is understood by some monks some of the time. I don't think the reason is too far to be sought; it is because we are citizens of a democracy. Naturally we will bring our basic political ideas and instincts to the monastic chapter. This is to be expected. We are not children with no ideas or aspirations, and we have certain desires about how things should be decided. As I said earlier, I am not one of those who is comfortable with the oft-heard canard that "the church is not a democracy." In fact, some of our democratic tendencies are very useful in the chapter or the senior council.

First of all, the very idea of *each* monk being responsible for the arrangements of the affairs of the community is a precious democratic instinct. We are not a herd of sheep who prefer that someone else decide things for us. It is *our* community, and we must take responsibility for it by our willingness to participate. That last word is crucial, of course. Participatory democracy is something this country is built on, and when it fades from sight—when people cannot bother to vote, for example—we are in trouble. The same goes for the monastic chapter. We have to be ready to pay our dues.

Strange as it may seem, not all monastic communities really buy into this idea. For whatever reasons, they prefer to remain passive in the face of important questions. This lack of interest in helping to decide matters can result from many different causes. For example, a dominating superior who reigns supreme for decades can virtually take the air out of the room for the community. They lose interest in participating because they have seen that their opinions are really not valued and are usually ignored. After a while the place becomes an autocracy with only one full-fledged moral agent, namely, the superior.

But it is not only tyranny that can create this kind of apathy. Sometimes a community appears on the surface to be fairly normal, with ideas and opinions like everyone else, yet when you get them into the chapter meeting and confront them with actual decisions, they beg off. They do not wish to have input on important matters. They prefer to let the boss decide. Of course, if they have to vote by secret ballot they will do it, but as far as expressing definite opinions, forget it. Moreover, they do not even want to *think* about the hard questions. Indeed, that could be an important part of the problem, namely, moral laziness. It is, after all, fairly hard work to operate as a responsible adult. It is much easier to snooze away in the passive doldrums.

RB 3 does not seem to expect this kind of passivity when the monks are consulted by the abbot. Here is what it says: "The brothers, however, should offer their advice with all deference and humility, and not presume to assert their views in a bold manner" (3.4). Another comment along the same lines goes like this: "Let no one in the monastery pursue a personal agenda, nor should anyone presume to argue impudently with his abbot." In both cases it is obvious that Benedict is worrying about aggressive behavior by the monks. Apparently he was dealing with people who had no particular doubts about their self-worth and were not afraid to let authority know what they thought. It sounds as if they were fairly combative.

Everyone knows that humility is a primary value in the Benedictine Rule, so it is not surprising he should invoke it at this point. The term "deference of humility" is even stronger. It warns the monk not to express his opinion in order to somehow bulldoze the way to what he wants. Another typical Benedictine word is "presume." Presumption is something Benedict cannot stand because it indicates that the monk does not know his place. And what is his place in the chapter meeting? He is not an advocate, at least in the sense of somehow forcing others into his way of thinking. He is simply asked for his opinion about something. He is not asked to make a speech that will influence the other monks into a certain way of thinking. He may well be persuasive, but that is not what he sets out to do. He just puts his opinion out there for people to hear. They can take it or leave it. It is of no ultimate concern to him whether they agree with him or not. Once he has expressed himself, he has done his job. And once the discussion is over and the abbot decides what should be done, he accepts it in obedience. This is a special kind of obedience. It may well involve swallowing your own ideas or even admitting you were wrong. But the point is that after you have expressed your opinion the matter is out of your hands.

At this point someone might well react with the rejoinder that all of this is fine but it is simply at variance with the way things are decided in a democracy. In our system things are basically fought out in a kind of verbal combat that often lacks most of the refinements of Benedict's chapter 3.

Even at the highest levels, such as the Congress, verbal polemics are the norm, not humble, sweet charity. To ask people to put aside their fighting instincts seems unreasonable. Besides, it will be said, people tend to form partisan groups that then contend with each other. That same thing could very well happen in the monastic chapter, at least over some questions.

This sort of thing does not seem very common in current monastic life, but it was not all that uncommon in the pioneer stages of Benedictine life in this country. Some of the minutes and records of early chapter meetings indicate that people back then were not afraid to express rather strong opinions. Verbal battles were not considered shocking or even out of place. Clearly, much of this depended on the general level of the culture. The American frontier was a rough and ready place in which there was little room for subtlety or nicety.

I myself got a jolt many years ago when my uncle, who was a monk about twenty-five years my senior, said to me: "You know, I don't understand you young guys today. Years ago we used to have some real fights. We would have it out in public, throw furniture at each other. But you guys are like a bunch of angora cats!" This was quite a statement, because he was a man who was dying of a brain tumor. He had had surgery that resulted in the loss of some inhibitions, so he had no hesitation is letting people know how he felt in his last few weeks and months. He could see that life was becoming less spontaneous and frank among us, and he thought that was a loss.

By and large I think it *is* a loss. We still have to be willing to express our honest opinion about things. But the situation in the monastic chapter is a special one, and it calls for special parameters. There is no room for a fistfight in the monastic chapter, but neither is there any gain if people will not say what they think and feel. Still, they have to do so in a proper and decent manner. Unfortunately, this is almost impossible for some people. For various reasons they cannot express themselves calmly and objectively in public. It is a skill they have never learned, and maybe they cannot learn it because of their temperament. It could be that they cannot speak at all in groups of more than a few people. So be it.

I would think, however, that the basic difference between a democratic advocacy meeting and the monastic chapter lies in the basic assumptions of each situation. The main concern in the democratic process is to *prevail*. People want their interests and concerns to prevail over those of others. There may be some pious talk about the common good, but all too often it is mainly a matter of *winning*. That certainly goes for elections, and it also seems to be the concern in decision-making on a regular basis. Sometimes, of course, we want to promote our ideal because we think it is best for the common good. But all too often we just want what we want. That seems to be the tone of too much recent American politics.

The monastic chapter, however, is concerned with something very different, namely, the will of God. The basic question before the group is never just pragmatic: Should we pave this road or not? Rather, what does God want us to do in this situation? If we lose sight of the faith dimension it is not long before things spin out of focus and we are simply pushing for what we want. The will of God is not always so clear for the many issues we must decide, yet we are not thereby excused from seeking to know the divine will in all matters. We have no guarantee we will always correctly discern God's will for us, but if we are at least trying, we have some chance to do so.

Chapter Four   *Paternalism*

When we speak of paternalism, a fundamental distinction needs to be kept in mind. In our time the word usually has a pejorative meaning, referring to an authority that intrudes too readily into the private lives of those who do not necessarily want that kind of attention. But Webster also speaks of another kind of paternalism, namely, the kind of authority that wishes to care for the personal lives of its subjects. By and large, people in every age want their superiors to care about them as persons.

Benedict's Paternalism

The paternalism of the Rule of Benedict, of course, is centered on the person of the abbot. This figure, who is the head of the cenobitic community, appears already in chapter 2 of the Holy Rule. This prominent position is partly due to the fact that in the first chapters of his document Benedict is copying from the Rule of the Master. Yet it would not have to have been that way. For example, both the Rule of Basil and the Rule of Augustine, ancient monastic Rules well known and respected by Benedict, hardly mention the superior until the last chapters, and even then the superior does not have a very dominant place in those Rules.

Not only does Benedict's abbot appear early, he shows up almost everywhere in the Holy Rule. A mere count of the incidence of the Latin term *abbas* makes this plain, for it occurs in forty-four out of seventy-three chapters. What is more, it is used over a hundred times throughout the Rule. When we take into account the other terms for the superior, and also the indirect references, the number of usages is huge. There is no doubt that the Rule of Benedict is heavily based on the person of the superior.

Not only is Benedict's abbot everywhere, he is also rather overwhelming. The portrait the author creates in RB 2 sets the abbot on a high pedestal where he controls every aspect of the life of the monastic community. On the other hand, Benedict makes sure that the abbot understands well that he is not an autocrat who can do as he pleases. The abbot is told to keep in mind that he will one day have to stand before the judgment seat of Almighty God, where he will be judged not only for his own conduct but for that of his disciples (RB 2.37-38).

When we compare this chapter with the corresponding treatise in the Rule of the Master from which it is adapted (RM 2), we find to our surprise that Benedict's treatment is even harsher than that of the Master. This effect may not be intended by Benedict, who seems to want to shorten the Master's long treatment. Unfortunately, however, Benedict has left out some of the gentler and more attractive comments by the Master, giving us a rather austere and almost crushing picture of monastic authority.

Another aspect of Benedict's paternalism lies in his presentation of the abbot as a sort of micro-manager. Nowadays, of course, leaders are criticized for meddling in minor matters they should be delegating to their subordinates. But in Benedict's mind there do not appear to be any such matters: his abbot is expected to manage every aspect of community life. Thus in RB 32 we find the abbot dispensing the tools for the daily labor, and at the end of the day he receives them back and notes well what is missing. Elsewhere, in RB 38.6, the abbot is told to watch carefully to see when the monks need more food because of circumstances.

One situation in which we might expect the abbot to assume a lower profile is in community meetings. He is instructed to call all the monks together for consultation and to listen carefully to each one of them, even the least prestigious such as the novices (RB 3). Yet a closer examination of this chapter shows that it hardly describes a democratic process. The abbot is in complete charge: he sets the agenda, he controls the discussion, and he makes the final decision. This may not be the way all modern communities handle their meetings, but it is the way Benedict wants them run.

A quotation from RB 44 on "how the excommunicated should make satisfaction" shows again how central the abbot is to the details of everyday life:

> When he has been bidden by the abbot, (the monk) should come and prostrate at the feet of the abbot himself and then of all, that they might

pray for him. Then, if the abbot commands it, he should be received back
to his place in choir, or to the place decided by the abbot. He should not,
however, presume to perform a psalm or lesson or anything else unless
again the abbot gives the order.

This is a particularly vivid case of Benedict's abbot-centeredness, but it is
by no means uncharacteristic of the Rule.

In RB 31, Benedict shows us an official who obviously has been delegated a good deal of authority by the abbot. The cellarer is the manager
of the temporal goods of the community and especially the distribution
of food. Benedict also makes it clear that the cellarer must be not only a
good manager but a mature spiritual person. "He should be a wise person,
of mature character and well disciplined. He should not be gluttonous,
arrogant, violent, unfair, stingy, or wasteful. Rather, he should be one who
fears God and is like the father to the whole community" (RB 31.1-2).

Yet even this very important lieutenant of the abbot is tightly circum-
scribed with warnings about the limits of his authority. Far from being an
autonomous figure of authority, he is told over and over that he is strictly
subordinate to the abbot's orders, from which he must not deviate in the
least. "Let him care well for all that the abbot commits to him, but let him
not presume to meddle with what he withholds from him." In the course of
history some monasteries grew into vast economic entities, far larger than
any one man could manage. In those cases it was not unusual for cellarers
to forget that the abbot is in charge of everything in Benedict's monastery.

When we discuss the subordinate officials Benedict wants to have put
in place we are broaching the question of delegation. Anybody who has
some experience of how a larger organization must function knows the
need for the top official to impart some of his own power to his subordinates, for the good of the group and for her own well-being. To judge
from Benedict's remarks about the installation of deans in RB 21, he seems
to have understood this issue quite well: "Only those should be chosen
deans with whom the abbot can confidently share his burdens" (RB 21.3).
Clearly they must be trusted, and they must be trustworthy.

Another glimpse of Benedict's delegation of authority can be found
in RB 46.5-6. The author is dealing with the delicate question of hidden
spiritual faults and sins. How are they to be healed? How are people to be
reconciled? "If, however, it is a question of a hidden problem of conscience,
the monk should only reveal it to the abbot or one of the spiritual seniors.
For they know how to cure their own wounds and those of others, without
divulging them in public." Benedict seems to admit that no matter how
important the abbot's spiritual leadership is to the community it probably

cannot accommodate all persons and all situations. Monks should be free to choose their own spiritual director, and such a person is to be considered a spiritual authority in the monastery.

For the modern reader who expects collaboration among leaders in most situations these somewhat minimal instances of delegation of authority in the Rule of Benedict may not seem too significant. But when we lay this Rule against its principal template, namely, the Rule of the Master, the thing looks different. If there is anything lacking in that earlier monastic Rule it is precisely delegation of authority. What the Master presents instead is an omnicompetent abbot who controls all aspects of community life and needs no assistance in his supervision.

The problem is not that the Master makes no provision for subordinate officials. Indeed, he has basically the same set of secondary officers as does Benedict: deans, cellarer, guest masters, and so on. The sad reality is that these people have no real *authority*. When we study what the Master has to say about these various roles it is obvious that what he wants are mere functionaries and not real authorities. This comes through in the way he employs them as mere watchdogs and not true leaders on any level. Furthermore, he indicates his fundamental disdain for his subordinates by constantly warning them against abuse of their functions. We have seen that Benedict also has this tendency, but not to the extent that it shows up in the Rule of the Master.

In our opening statement we noted that "paternalism" need not have a negative meaning; it can refer to a type of leadership that emphasizes the care of individual persons beside and perhaps above institutional concerns. Overall, it can be said that this is one of the strongest aspects of Benedict's abbot: he knows the monks and he takes care of them.

This element can be inferred from the title Benedict confers on the superior, namely, *abbas* or father. This appellation is so familiar to us that we hardly give it a second glance. Actually Benedict explains it rather obscurely as a title of Christ. But first of all we need to recall what a father is. A father is someone who has a child and who cares for that child. The relationship is not just juridical; it is highly personal. We have always known how important it is for mental and emotional health to begin life supported by loving parents. Psychologists now tell us it is virtually irreplaceable. Of course, the monastery is not a biological family, and not all abbots are able to offer warm, personal affirmation to all their subjects. In fact, Benedict seems to avoid the use of the term "son" for the monk, even though it is very frequent in the Rule of the Master. Still, the Rule shows the abbot exercising direct, personal care for the monks in many situations.

Indeed, Benedict seems to have realized that his initial treatise on the abbot (RB 2), which we have already described as quite formidable, is not adequate. To supplement that towering view of the superior he crafted a second essay on the abbot that is much more pastoral in tone. Here is a typical passage from RB 64:

> Let him always be wary of his own brittleness, and remember not to break the bent reed. . . . He should aim more at being loved than feared. He should not be restless and troubled, not extreme and headstrong, not jealous and over-suspicious; for then he will have no peace. And whether it is a question of spiritual or material matters he should give prudent and moderate orders. (RB 64.13, 15)

This kind of gentle advice, which is actually based on the writings of St. Augustine, essentially goes back to the New Testament. Moreover, it is ultimately based on the Suffering Servant from Isaiah, the primary Old Testament image by which Jesus understood his ministry. When an abbot is tempted to use his power in a rough manner he should remember that his basic model is Jesus himself, who refused to return evil for evil even in the face of unjust authority.

If Benedict's abbot is primarily nonviolent, he is also bent on the mission of reconciliation and forgiveness. The place where this comes out most graphically is probably RB 27, on "the abbot's preoccupation with the excommunicated." Someone who objects to this as an exaggerated over-translation should be informed that it is justified by the first verse that follows it: "The abbot should focus all his attention on the care of the wayward brothers." Apart from the practical difficulty of putting all his efforts into the rehabilitation of the troubled brother, it should be noted that Jesus was looking in the same direction when he stated categorically: "It is not the healthy who need a physician, but the sick" (Mark 2:17).

As RB 27 goes on to explain, however, the sick in this case, that is, the excommunicated, may not welcome the ministrations of the abbot. Indeed, they may be locked in a struggle against his authority so that he finds himself unable to help them in a direct fashion. Then Benedict suggests he send in other officials who may have better access to the resistant member. Even then he does not want the "*senpect*" or delegate to conspire with the culprit, but simply to offer a less threatening form of authority in that situation. In my view this is one of the most remarkable instances of Benedict's deep understanding of the real function of paternal authority. It does not stand on its dignity; it may have to resort to indirect means to achieve its ends; it is primarily concerned with the salvation of the individual, not the prestige of the institution.

This same kind of tough but gentle care and concern is also prominent in the next chapter of the Benedictine penal code, namely, RB 28. Here we have a situation in which a monk has fallen back into behavior that renders him "excommunicated." The author talks about the various means the abbot might use to heal a seriously troubled member. The whole discussion is couched in symbolic medical language, so it is not easy to tell exactly what Benedict has in mind. But one thing is sure: such a case merits the abbot's fullest attention. He cannot excuse himself on the grounds that one problematic member should not take up all his time. That is no way to run a railroad.

Indeed it is not, and it reminds us that the monastery is not a "railroad" or General Motors or any other kind of impersonal institution. It is a gathering of individual persons, all of whom are irreplaceable members of the body of Christ and made in the image and likeness of God. We live in a complicated world nowadays, one in which the abbot often has multiple practical concerns, dozens of meetings to attend. Nevertheless, in the face of all these things the abbot must hold firmly in mind that his role is primarily pastoral. Unlike some modern religious congregations, we are not ruled by committee. As some wag once pointed out: "A committee does not have a soul to save or a butt to kick." That does not apply to abbots.

It would not be right to leave this topic without saying something about one of Benedict's most tender and personal chapters, namely, the care of the sick (RB 36). Scholars of early monastic institutions have pointed out that Benedict actually created the first monastic infirmary, and perhaps the prototype for modern hospitals. He arranges for a separate room for the sick and he also institutes a special office of *servitor* (servant) of the sick. We now call this official the "infirmarian," but we should remember that this monk or nun does not have the ultimate responsibility for the care of the sick. That still belongs to the abbot. "The abbot must be very careful that (the sick) suffer no neglect whatever." "The abbot should be extremely careful that the sick not be neglected by the cellarers or servers."

One might be excused for wondering why the abbot should appoint nurses if he himself is still responsible. The reason is closely connected to the positive element of Benedict's paternalism: the individual monk or nun is the primary concern of the abbot. Essentially, he cannot delegate this responsibility and this relationship. If the community becomes so large that he does not know all the members, or cannot take care of them, that community is *too* large. One should not have to make an appointment to see the abbot weeks in advance. Benedictine authority is "hands-on" or it is dysfunctional.

Contemporary Considerations

In the first part of this essay we indicated that we think the Rule of Benedict is too "abbot-centered." That should not be taken as a claim that we are currently plagued with overweening monastic authority. In fact, at least to judge from the situation in the United States, that is not at all the case. On the contrary, it is generally agreed that we currently suffer from a crisis of authority in that we do not have *enough* of it. Sometimes when contemporary monasteries come to elect an abbot or a prioress they find that nobody is capable of monastic leadership or nobody is willing to take the job. In that case someone has to be found in another abbey to come and take over, but that merely moves the problem of dearth of leadership back one notch.

One possible explanation for this very worrisome situation is that leadership is not being actively fostered. That can happen when top authority is so jealous of its own turf that instead of encouraging other members to develop leadership skills it actively undermines them. That is never done overtly, of course, because the scandal would be too great. But it can happen subtly, and if it goes on for enough years the result is a kind of vacuum in which no one is prepared to take over when the abbot resigns. Indeed, some abbots are good at almost everything—except nurturing and developing other leaders in the monastery. They have defaulted on one of their principal tasks.

It is probably also the case that our society is not particularly conducive to the development of strong leaders. It has been pointed out in regard to Generation X (persons born between 1963 and 1982) that they are characteristically allergic to roles of top leadership. According to the same report the general feeling with these people is that such roles involve too much stress and conflict. Hence they would prefer to fit into medium-level roles that enable them to maintain smooth personal relationships. These people are surely right in fearing that leadership can mean conflict. The reason is simple: some people resent authority and are always at odds with it. This means that whoever is in the abbot's or prioress's office will be the object of dislike and even hatred by some members. This is simply a byproduct of Original Sin.

But the community still needs leadership and someone must exercise it, often at considerable personal cost. There is a parable in the book of Judges (chap. 9) about the time when the trees of the forest came to choose a leader. When they offered the job to the noblest and most beautiful trees, all of them turned it down. Finally they came to the bramble, the roughest and least attractive tree of them all. The bramble knew that everybody else had turned the job down, but it accepted the task. It also warned the other trees that they could expect the only kind of leadership the bramble could manage, given its nature: harsh treatment.

In modern monasteries, which are light-years apart from the primitive rural situation found in Judges, we may still observe the same phenomenon. Because many communities are involved in complex, sophisticated projects such as colleges or hospitals, any number of their monks and nuns have some experience of leadership on the secular level. This sometimes makes them attractive candidates for the job of abbot or prioress. But to take such a job can be a decisive break in one's career. It may also mean that a person may never be able to resume his or her career path. One man I know was elected abbot in the middle of his studies for a Ph.D. at one of the country's best universities. He gave up his academic future to serve the community, but not all monks are willing to do so.

Apart from the general shortage of natural leaders in our monasteries at this time, it should also be noted that monks and nuns today are usually not entirely comfortable with the profile of the abbot given in the Holy Rule. Since we live in very different circumstances than sixth-century Italy it is no surprise that we have a different sensibility. In a sense nothing has changed: we still need strong leaders. But we don't want to be dominated by overwhelming authority. Although a few communities still seem to thrive under such leadership, it may be questioned whether they are actually healthy. Recent history has featured whole nations virtually worshiping monstrous leaders such as Hitler and Stalin, which is a frightening subject for meditation.

By and large, modern nuns and monks want to be involved in collaborative leadership. They want to have a say in the decisions that most affect their lives. Again, this can be ridiculed as a mere pathology of democracy, but in fact it was the normal condition in the early church. The autocracy of feudalism and the Middle Ages that shaped modern church history moved in a different direction. The aftermath of Vatican II shows that this problem is by no means solved. No matter how many council documents urge the full participation of all members in the affairs of the church, the drift since 1965 has been back toward top-down authority.

We can be thankful that the typical monastic community will no longer put up with autocratic behavior on the part of its leaders, and the average abbot or prioress understands this well enough. They generally find ways to exercise real authority while remaining open to the input of all their members. This does not mean that there are no longer instances of abuse of authority by monastic leaders. Sometimes the community simply elects the wrong person; sometimes the pressures of the job wind up destroying the superior. The problem is not always "paternalism" as such, but various other aberrations.

One final point may be made in this admittedly rambling essay, and that is this: men and women seem to want different qualities in their leaders. To risk a gross simplification, women want more personal attention and men want less. That seems to indicate that "maternalism" is less obnoxious than "paternalism." This generalization will not of course apply to *all* women or men, but overall it seems true enough. I do not know how this works out in vast modern Orders with "leadership teams," but presumably they find some way to make their sisters feel personally cared for.

Chapter Five

The Idolatry of Security

9/11 and All That

One of the defining events of recent times was the attack on the World Trade Center and the Pentagon on September 11, 2001. This was one of those historical traumas that sear our consciousness to the point that everyone knows what they were doing that morning about 9 a.m. EDT. Of course, it was a scenario ready made for television. Who can forget the live coverage of the towers falling down? In fact, many people thought they were watching a science fiction film until it dawned on them that it was a real-life happening.

Among the many reasons why the attacks were so horrifying was the simple fact that they impacted a couple of our main social institutions, namely, the New York financial district and the Washington military-industrial complex. If you want to stir up a hornet's nest, just mess with American finance and the military. In that sense it was no great surprise that the government immediately declared war on the Arab terrorists and retaliated with attacks on Afghanistan and Iraq. No doubt this satisfied the longing of many people for retribution.

For students of world culture the events of 9/11 are even more significant, for they symbolize a long-simmering feud between Islamic fundamentalism and Western imperialism. There was and is a great deal of resentment in the Arab world against American pop culture, which they think has a very corrosive effect on their youth and which they have a hard time excluding. As for the youth, they both hate and love our movies and our MTV, but they are also extremely frustrated by their inability to enjoy the high material culture they see on American television. The more highly educated they become, the more they resent their lack of opportunities for good jobs in the Arab countries.

From our point of view the 9/11 attack was particularly devastating to the American need for material security. It is no secret that many people find extremely unsettling the idea that a handful of Arab extremists could strike at the heart of our country. Immediately there was talk about the vulnerability of our whole infrastructure. Who is protecting our water supply, our bridges, our electrical grid? Suddenly it dawned on us that we might not be as safe and sound as we always thought we were.

This virtual meltdown of the American psyche was no doubt part of the whole purpose of the attack. People in the Third World are quite well aware of how attached Americans are to their material security. There was wild rejoicing in the streets of Karachi and Kabul at the television pictures of American terror that day, which of course further enraged some Americans. But we should remember that those people live with that kind of insecurity *all the time*. For them a few thousand dead and wounded is just a normal day's events. For example, two million people have been killed in the civil war in the Eastern Congo, a war that barely makes our newspapers any more.

Politically speaking, the demolition of the Twin Towers and the Pentagon was a sort of gift from the gods for the administration in Washington. From then on George W. Bush and Dick Cheney could more or less write their own ticket in the name of national security. Certainly some of the steps they took were justified. By and large, people do not object to being thoroughly frisked in airports and at customs. But when it comes to the permanent detention of suspects and the torture of prisoners, then we begin to wonder. At what point do we put our foot down and say, "Enough! We won't have that, even in the name of national security!"?

Living in a Safe, Insured World

Part of the background of our fervent devotion to material security in this country is our insurance system. Of course this is not a new invention. Sophisticated societies have always had some form of insurance, and even impoverished ones have their own methods, such as large families to cushion the dangers of old age for the parents. No matter what form it takes, insurance is always an attempt to eliminate the unacceptable risks of life. But that begs the question of what risks are truly unacceptable, a judgment that varies widely from culture to culture.

The possibility of factoring out risk from life was greatly enhanced by the advent of modern science. One of the main advantages of good science is that it enables us to control certain aspects of our environment and thus protect ourselves from dangerous risks. It is sometimes hard to remember that until fairly recently there was nothing anybody could do about many diseases. I know that I personally have been saved by scientific medicine from almost sure death at least half a dozen times. And that kind of control now extends to many aspects of material existence.

Given our success in taming nature "red in tooth and claw," we have gradually developed a mentality that begins to assume that *all* risks are unacceptable. We have become quite aggressive, even belligerent, at pursuing our "rights" in the face of life's nasty surprises. Not only do we use insurance for this purpose, we also use litigation. If something dreadful happens to us we immediately look for someone to blame and sue. Since we assume that life should be risk-free, *somebody* must be to blame when that proves to be untrue. But of course the more we sue each other, the higher our insurance premiums escalate. You can't have one without the other.

One more footnote before we close this section. I think one of the prices we pay for our idolatry of security is that we now have a pretty flat and anodyne society. Many people find modern life quite boring. I think this is the root cause of the pleasure so many people seem to take from gambling. No risk, no rush. And that is also the reason some people pursue some extreme sports that one can only watch with horror when one clicks on the wrong TV channel. What is more, I think boredom is a very important issue in the life of monks. After all, Michael Casey was not afraid to entitle a book on monasticism *The Unexciting Life.*

Benedict's Teaching on Monastic Security

When we approach the Rule of St. Benedict with questions about security we might begin with the notion of death. Since it is the ultimate physical threat, death is really at the core of human insecurity. Unless we commit suicide we do not know when we will die, nor do we really know how. It is the very uncertainty of the thing that makes us uneasy. Most people are not paralyzed by the fear of death, but we all know that we must remain somehow aware of it if we are not to stumble into it in a tragic way.

What does Benedict say about death? Surprisingly little. One of the very few mentions of death in the Holy Rule occurs in a series of aphorisms called "the instruments of good works" (RB 4). Here is the saying, along with a bit of context: "Fear judgment day. Have a healthy fear of hell. Long for eternal life with the desire of the Holy Spirit. Keep your eye on death every day" (RB 4.44-47). A glance at this series of admonitions makes it obvious that the real worry is not physical but spiritual death. This cluster of warnings, which actually occurs at least four times in RB (4.44-47; 7.10-13; 7.26-30; 19.1-3) is one of the rather sober themes Benedict seems to have drawn from the Rule of Basil. Apparently it is one of Benedict's favorite lessons.

In fact, it was a lesson the ancient monks learned well. They were justly famous for their unflinching focus on death, which they insisted on contemplating in their life of prayer. The medieval painters loved to show the old monks gazing at a human skull they kept on their table. If anybody doubts that such a thing was possible, I invite you to go to St. Catherine's monastery on Mount Sinai, where they will show you their charnel house in which the skulls of their departed confrères are cheerfully piled in the corner.

In contrast to this, we have to admit that our own society is decidedly squeamish about the sight of death and the corpses of the dead. As much as we can, we keep dying people out of sight and we also cosmeticize corpses to seem as alive as possible. God forbid that one of our children should see somebody die or should see a dead body! We recently had a candidate who even professed shock that we would dump dead calves on the ground outside the corral during calving. He worried, he said, that some kid from town might catch sight of one of those dead beasts.

At any rate, it does not seem that Benedict is particularly concerned about the process of physical death. He does provide a decent infirmary, but not out of any morbid fear of death. What concerns him is the tragic possibility that we might end up in the torment of the everlasting death called hell. Benedict is not like modern preachers, who seem to want to spare their listeners that kind of grim prospect. The pendulum has swung so far that many parents do not want their children hearing about such things in church or Sunday school. Again, spare the children! But Benedict refuses to spare the monks.

Yet the issue of security goes beyond the fear of death. What kind of attitude did Benedict have toward the risks of life in his time? Before we look in the Rule on that question it might be good to recall the general state of Italy in the sixth century. When we do that we find that Benedict lived in some very rough times. On top of the usual problems of ancient populations in the face of famine, plague, and natural disasters, Italy in the period 530–550 was ravaged by continual warfare between the Byzantine and Gothic armies. And if Benedict lived at Monte Cassino we can be sure that he and his monks suffered the impact of war in a direct way, for that hill has always been a prime military target. Indeed, we know that his monastery was totally destroyed by the Lombards soon after his death, and many times since.

When we look in the Rule for traces of this social upheaval we don't find too much, but there are a couple of intriguing passages that might give us pause. For example, in RB 40.8-9, on the quantity of drink, this is what he has to say: "When, though, local conditions are such that not even the amount of wine mentioned above can be obtained, but much less or none at all, those who live there should bless God and not murmur. Most of all we warn them to avoid murmuring."

This may not strike us as a particularly significant passage for our purposes here. But anybody who has lived in Italy for any amount of time will know that it is more serious than it looks at first sight. Why? Because in Italy wine is not a luxury; it is a necessity. Or at least the Italians think so. As with all Mediterranean people, they use wine as a regular part of their diet. For them to be without wine is a real hardship, almost a calamity. But Benedict lets them know that it is not the end of the world. They won't die if they have to drink water. Another passage of the same type is found in RB 48.7-9, where we read this:

> If, however, the necessities of the place or poverty demand that they themselves work at the harvest, they should not be sad. For if they live by the work of their hands, then they are true monks, as were our Fathers and the Apostles. Yet everything should be arranged in moderation because of the faint-hearted.

In a way the message of these two passages is very similar. If certain things turn out to be inconvenient, even very inconvenient, do not throw up your hands or collapse. It appears that Benedict's monks were not used to the very hard physical work of harvesting. After all, in the sixth century that was mostly peasant labor, the kind of thing Roman gentlemen avoided at all costs. But Benedict tells his monks they may find it necessary to roll up their sleeves and do some of that work.

And if they do, he assures them, they will not be doing anything so heroic. After all, he says, this kind of work was common for "our Fathers and the Apostles." Now I do not know exactly what apostles he is referring to, but the gospels do not show the Twelve doing much hard work. Of course, they were commercial fishermen and that is not child's play. But hard labor is not much of an evangelical value. As for the "Fathers," he may be thinking of the desert monks, who used to hire themselves out for harvesting in the Nile valley. Still, it was the Cistercians, not the Benedictines, who first tried to make hard physical labor an integral part of the monastic life. I am not sure they succeeded.

But my point here is more general. It seems to me that Benedict is simply letting the monks know they have no guarantee of a convenient life. Certainly most of their neighbors at Monte Cassino did not. Sometimes life is harsh and burdensome. Monks should not be looking for a soft and cushy life: three hots and a cot, as it were. There was a time, in the 1930s, when some people did indeed come to American monasteries looking for some security against extreme hardship. That has not been the case lately, but it could happen again. Benedict insists that the monks must grow up. Adults expect that life will sometimes be very hard.

Still, after all this talk about the pitfalls of looking for too much security in this world it must still be admitted that people do need *some* security. For example, child psychologists are now well aware of the damage inflicted on infants and young children when they are deprived of the material and emotional support they need for normal development. They tell us that this is a deficit that cannot be made up in later life.

But older people can also manifest the scars of unmet needs. When I first came to the monastery I noticed that a few of our older monks seemed never to feel a sense of material security. When the community discussed building plans or other extraordinary expenses in the chapter meeting these men would typically express anxiety about whether we really had the money for such risky outlays, and no amount of assurance by the treasurer could ease their fears. Over the years I learned that some of these monks had in fact been traumatized in the same 1930s when the rest of the nation suffered in the Great Depression. For example, one monk told me that he was a pastor in a remote parish and his car was falling apart. But when he wrote to the abbot he was told that there was simply no money for another car. Another man told me that he was not allowed to take books from the library to his parish in the boondocks. The unfortunate result of this kind of penury was that these monks learned to "take care of themselves." They also learned never to fully trust the community again.

Does the Rule of Benedict speak to this situation? I think it does. For example, in RB 55.17-19 we read the following:

> If someone is found to have something he has not received from the abbot, he should undergo very severe discipline. But to completely root out this vice of private ownership, the abbot must provide people with everything they need: that is, cowl, tunic, sandals, shoes, belt, knife, stylus, needle, handkerchief, writing tablets. This should remove all pretext of want.

It is important here get past a couple of distractions. First, the incredibly simple list of what a sixth-century monk would need should not bemuse us. Nowadays it might well include a personal computer, a credit card, an automobile, and so forth. Times change. Second, the idea that absolutely all private ownership is to be abolished should not shock us. If we are monks we know that this kind of ideal is not impossible to live with. In fact, most of us do not consider it much of a hardship. Of course, we may interpret it a bit more broadly than Benedict would have liked . . . .

But the important thing to remember here is simply this: if monks are not to have personal possessions, then they must be taken care of. There are two sides to this coin. The monk's part, which is heavily emphasized in RB 33, is to avoid the vice of avarice. Normally this means undue attachment to worldly goods, but for the Benedictine monk it means attachment to *any* material chattels. Yet Benedict makes it clear enough that he considers this to be merely the outward, symbolic aspect of the monastic need to let go of self-will. Indeed, he puts it in the plainest form possible: "They have neither their bodies nor their own wills at their own disposal" (RB 33.4).

RB 55, however, takes care of the other side of the equation. It is addressed to the abbot, and it urges him to make sure the monks get what they need for their well-being. His role as the steward of monastic poverty is not just to make sure no monk is amassing private goods. True, Benedict does tell the abbot to check the mattresses to see whether things are being hidden there (RB 55.16)! But again we should not be distracted by this stipulation that is so foreign to our mentality. The main point is that the abbot must take good care of his monks.

Of course, this last sentence could sound a bit paternalistic. One of the things some monasteries changed after Vatican II was the handling of personal money. Especially among the Sisters it was felt that the system of asking for permissions on an *ad hoc* basis had resulted in economic infantilism among the members. So in order to promote fiscal maturity, individuals were given a monthly stipend from which they had to take care of their incidental personal expenses. Some communities went so far as to require an annual budget in advance. Needless to say, such an arrangement has a way of focusing the attention.

But is it what Benedict had in mind? And does it really promote what the monastic life is supposed to be all about? I have friends in the "world" who think we are rather foolish when we institute this kind of personal budgeting. They tell me: You joined the monastery to worry about the things of God. Why burden yourself with this kind of trivial stuff? We would absolutely love to get clear of this kind of nickel-and-diming!

This was also the thinking of John Cassian, that redoubtable fifth-century philosopher of the monastic life. When in *Conference* 19.6 he calls the monastic life "a life free from care," he means precisely that a cenobitic monk should not have to worry about the nuts and bolts of everyday mundane existence. That should be taken care of by the abbot or the business manager. The individual monk should be free to devote his attention to what really counts for a monk, namely, the contemplative life. All that time and energy other people spend on their budgets and taxes and so on should be spent on the things of God.

But how far do you carry this kind of thinking? If the monks should be free from care, should the whole community also cast its care on the Lord, even in material matters? For example, should the monks have health insurance? Recently a candidate for our monastery told me that he did not think so. He asked me how we could square this with monastic poverty. Of course he had put his finger on a difficult point. Our community is currently spending fully one-third of our entire budget on health insurance. Years ago we had no health insurance at all. Recently I asked an old monk who had been procurator at that time what they did when a monk contracted a chronic illness. His answer was: "We prayed he would soon die."

Nowadays we do not feel quite comfortable with that answer. We do not feel that we can subject the whole community to the kind of risk that catastrophic illness could bring to us all. We are well aware that we are not alone in this dilemma. In fact, the whole American nation wonders what to do about skyrocketing health costs. The Clinton presidency was nearly ruined when he attempted to solve the problem. Fifteen years later the situation has become significantly worse, so much so that almost everybody is willing to consider some alternatives to what we now have.

The present dilemma of what to do about high-tech medicine is a direct byproduct of our insatiable, even idolatrous need for security. When people demand that the doctors explore every avenue in diagnosing and curing their health problems we end up with the exotic machinery and medicines we now have. But who is going to tell the doctor to forego some of this treatment? In fact the issue of security, whether against bombs or against disease, is not so easy to think through. St. Benedict had strong ideas on the subject, not all of which fit our time. But his basic teaching does fit all times and places: rely on the Lord! He alone is our security.

Chapter Six   *Work*

Many things found in the sixth-century Rule of Benedict have changed in the fifteen centuries since his time. One of those is work. It is not all that uncommon to find contemporary writers crediting Benedict with stimulating some important changes in the ancient attitude toward work. It is sometimes said that he played an important part in dignifying work and making it an essential aspect of a mature human existence. Some of this praise for Benedict's work ethic is encapsulated in the motto: "Work and Pray."

Work in the Holy Rule

Most of the teaching on work is found in RB 48, which is entitled "The Daily Manual Labor." That title is useful for our purposes here, but it is not entirely accurate. When we read through this rather long chapter we find that it is really about the entire monastic day and not just work. A rather elaborate timetable is laid out, giving precise demarcation for the hours of the Divine Office. Then the author instructs the monks to fill in the time between the hours with two activities, namely, work and *lectio divina*. So if we are in the business of crafting mottos perhaps we should settle on "pray, read, and work."

It must be admitted that the chapter starts off with a powerful statement about work: "Idleness is the soul's enemy, so therefore at determined times the brothers ought to be occupied with manual labor, and again at determined hours in *lectio divina*" (RB 48.1). Since idleness (*otiositas*) seems to be the opposite of work it is tempting to take this opening statement as a strong incitement to vigorous work for monks. No doubt it has some of that quality about it, but to understand the precise weight of the opening verse we need to compare Benedict's chapter 48 with the parallel chapter in the Rule of the Master (RM 50).

When we do that we find that the Master has a much longer and detailed diatribe against idleness, which he sees primarily as an opportunity for sin. In the eyes of the Master, work is mainly a means of keeping people occupied so that they do not fall into sin. Indeed, he tells the monks to come to each of the Little Hours full of gratitude that they have just spent another three-hour period free from sin. Besides lending a kind of hysterical atmosphere to the monastic day, this approach of the Master has the unfortunate effect of making work a mere stopgap against sin. It is hard to imagine a less attractive theology of work.

It might also be said that the Master is deathly afraid of *leisure* for his monks. The same cannot be said for Benedict. In fact, Benedict's basic vocabulary in this chapter reveals that he sees *lectio divina* itself as a form of leisure. Each time he comes to discuss that activity he introduces it this way: "Let them be free for *lectio divina*." The verb *vacare* is often translated "to devote oneself to," but the root meaning of *vaco* is to have some time and space that is free from constraint. In this case it might be said that the monks are to be free *from* work for at least three hours a day.

When a modern monk first encounters RB 48 in any serious fashion this great emphasis on *lectio divina* comes as a surprise. Typical contemporary Benedictine monasteries, and probably *most* monasteries throughout history, set aside little or no time for *lectio divina*. This is one of the great conundrums of Benedictine history. Why have the monks chosen to overlook this crucial element in Benedict's carefully balanced horarium? No doubt there were different reasons for different ages, but it is easy enough to imagine the current reason: three hours of prime time when the monks are not supposed to be working is a huge hole in the day. So clearly, any renewal of *lectio* is going to impact our work.

The plain fact is that in RB 48 work is not the major factor it is sometimes said to be. In simple quantitative terms Benedict wants his monks to work five or six hours a day, six days a week. Granted, that approximates the modern work week of forty hours, but it is nowhere near as much time as most Americans now spend working. Furthermore, we should not overlook the effect of the Day Hours of Terce, Sext, and None. When people are engaged in any kind of serious work, to break for even a few minutes to go to the chapel for common prayer is not a small thing. No doubt St. Benedict, who was simply following the majority of ancient monasteries, purposely *intended* the Little Hours to break into the workday. They were meant to assert the primacy of prayer over work. No, for Benedict, "work is not prayer!"

But in reality there are many kinds of work that cannot be interrupted without serious detriment. For example, most farm work and heavy labor demand long, unbroken hours of application. The simple problem of cleaning up makes it quite impossible to break every three hours for formal prayer. Even though Benedict claims in RB 48.8, "They are truly monks when they live by the work of their hands," and says this in regard to harvesting, the historical fact is that most monastic communities have found such work basically incompatible with the monastic horarium as outlined in RB 48. Even though Benedict claims that "our fathers and the apostles" lived by the work of their hands, one comes across precious little hard work in the Bible or the lives of the saints. In my estimation Benedict has crawled out on a rather slender branch with this claim for hard work.

The truth of this claim can easily be proven from Benedictine history. In the Middle Ages the monks found they could not make a living if they had to pray the entire Divine Office in the way Benedict prescribed. Around 1100 they came up with a solution of sorts by instituting the role of the "lay brothers." These people, who were invariably uneducated and joined the monastery as adults, were supposed to carry out the physical work of the monastery. They did not have the obligation to pray the Divine Office. In fact, they did not pronounce monastic vows. Normally they lived out on the various farms the monasteries gradually acquired and that provided the essential income of the community.

When the founders of the Cistercian reform set out to create a purification and renewal of Benedictine life, also about 1100, they were determined to do all the work themselves. That is, they could not see why choir monks could not also do enough physical work to maintain themselves. Within a few years they gave up their idealistic project as unfeasible. They brought in their own lay brothers, who became a major force in Cistercian history. Whether or not one regards this as some kind of failure, it seems to me proof that the Benedictine horarium, at least as it stands in RB 48, is essentially incompatible with many kinds of hard and serious work.

Of course there were other factors at work. For example, there is no question that most medieval monks or nuns came from the aristocratic class in Europe. As such they did not have a very positive attitude toward hard work. These were often people who were used to being waited on; in fact, many of them brought their own servants with them to the monastery! Also, there is no doubt that the upper classes in the Mediterranean world had a very jaundiced view of physical labor. That was something for slaves.

A free man or woman did not stoop to such things. St. Benedict may have wished to chip away at such attitudes in his Rule, but it is doubtful that he made much of a dent in the basic work ethic of his world.

In our own times no doubt, things have changed—but they have also stayed the same. For one thing, very few modern Benedictines come from such affluence that they have a disdain for physical work. At least in North America it is common for monks and nuns to engage in hard labor if the need arises. Actually, many North American monasteries have a long history of hard physical labor. The typical American abbey began in very modest circumstances; the monks had to roll up their sleeves and build their own buildings. Some of these monks are still alive, and they look back with nostalgia to the time when the whole community turned out for construction work in the summer. It was a time when everybody pitched in and contributed to the common work. In most cases those days are long past.

Still, when these same people try to live in other cultures, such as that of Latin America, it is considered something of a scandal if they actually get their hands dirty. The young novices coming into the monastery in such a culture are not eager for such work, especially in the sight of their peers. Moreover, nowadays building codes require us to hire specialists to do much of our construction.

At any rate, we still have to contend with the Benedictine horarium in regard to our work. For us the solution is not lay brothers. In fact, we now have only one class of monk. All of us pray the Divine Office together. But then how do we get the work done? By and large we simply modify the Office. We either gather the Little Hours into one bundle, thus removing them from the middle of the work periods, or we do away with them. In other words, we no longer struggle with the problem of the intrusive horarium. Benedict might not like our solution, but he did not have to live in the twenty-first century.

Contemporary Attitudes toward Work

When we turn our gaze to modern attitudes toward work we might characterize them as more serious than those of the ancient monks. Actually, it might be said that even in the context of its own times early monasticism had a rather cavalier attitude toward work. That is to say, the monks rarely if ever worked as hard as the real laborers in the society around them. I am not talking about the philosophers or the poets, but about the people who actually farmed the land, who actually built the buildings, and who actually maintained the roads. These are the real workers in every age. They do not speculate about the value of their work: they just do it.

Moreover, such work cannot be accomplished in dribs and drabs, a few hours at a time. That is good enough for hobbies but not for serious work. That kind of work takes all day. It typically begins at sunrise and it continues through the heat of the day until dark. Of course, much of the Western world now limits its work to eight hours a day, but that only came about because the industrial revolution subjected workers to killing conditions. For independent workers, longer days and weeks are often the norm even to this day. Work takes time, and it takes effort. It means showing up day after day whether you feel up to it or not.

Admittedly, this view of work is somewhat tied to the rural, non-industrial world. It applies mainly to jobs like farming and commercial fishing. It is certainly true of hand labor outdoors in any form, although work with machines can also be very demanding. But my point here is that such work has its own rhythms and demands. It especially has its seasons, which often take the form of a harvest to be gathered or a calf to be helped into the world. When these events occur the worker has to drop everything else and be present. When monks are involved in such things the neat and prim monastic schedule must give way to the necessities of nature, as it were.

Thus if monks want to farm they have to be ready to act like farmers. This is not hobby farming but the real thing: the calves that have to be delivered in an April blizzard, the hay that must be baled in the middle of a July night, the apples that must be picked before the first hard frost. Faced with work like this, monks can hire other people to do it or they can bend the monastic schedule to make these things possible. When the monks in France have to pick apples, for example, the only liturgy is held right out in the orchards. If the monks themselves want to engage in construction, they have to complete the concrete troweling before it dries. The Divine Office will have to wait. I don't think Benedict thought any differently about this, since he is forever moving the Office backward and forward to accommodate other exigencies (see RB 48).

Not all work is heavy labor, and in our machine and computer age less and less of it is such. But all serious work still takes time and has its own parameters. Most people who engage in scientific and/or intellectual work find it cannot be done well in short fragments. Much of this work demands continuity and even exclusivity. By that I mean that one must at least temporarily shut out all else in order to solve the problem or complete the thesis. People are different, of course, and some can actually work best in fragments. I once met a great scholar who loved to hop from project to project. He was easily bored, he said, and had no trouble locking in quickly on a new question. But for most of us that is not possible. We need whole mornings to write our books or solve our equations. A couple of hours between Sext and None are just not enough.

Furthermore, much work in our time demands extensive training. We now live in a world that does not easily tolerate amateurism even among monks. For example, somebody who has to handle expensive and complicated machinery simply has to be properly trained. This same thing goes for computers, of course, although many of us muddle along with insufficient knowledge of what we are doing with these amazing machines. It used to be that people were proud of being untrained because then they could appear as self-made men or women. Now, however, we want our nurses to be properly trained and our teachers to have learned intellectual discipline themselves before they are turned loose on us.

I don't want to run this thesis over a cliff. There is still plenty of room in society for the jack-of-all-trades and the handywoman. In fact, the American frontier was famous for producing those kinds of people. It was even said that the real advantage the American army had over any other army in the world wars was that every private could fix the engine in his own jeep. In the monastery we still have the need for skilled "maintenance monks" who can fix anything. One abbot was heard to lament: "I would trade four organists for one plumber!" Obviously it takes more training to be a good organist, but the point is that there is a limit to specialization.

To turn to a different aspect of work, it might be said that contemporary people seem to find their work much more engrossing and fascinating than did people in previous ages. For us today it is not enough that work puts bread on the table or that it just keeps us out of trouble. We want our work to be intrinsically interesting and rewarding. I do not use the word "rewarding" in the monetary sense. Many people today make plenty of money but are not happy with their work. Smart young people now routinely find extremely lucrative jobs in the world of finance or science and have no money worries. But is the job truly fulfilling?

Here again the point can be exaggerated. Hosts of people still have to do work that nobody could call fascinating. They need to do boring, dirty, sacrificial jobs because—they need a job. And society needs garbage collectors, factory workers, and so forth. They are extremely valuable and they deserve a living wage, and a good one. To be honest, we often find that these jobs are being done by the immigrant population, and especially the *illegal* immigrant population. These are the people who usually wind up doing the work educated Americans no longer are willing to do. They work in the slaughterhouses, the vegetable fields, and the sweat shops. So there are still plenty of punishing jobs in our world.

Even though we do not live in an ideal work world, people now often have higher aspirations than they did in former times. Many people in our Western society now see work as an important means of self-fulfillment. I do not mean this in a superficial or even selfish sense. Clearly most people work "to get ahead" in the sense of self-advancement. Some are more altruistic and consciously seek out jobs such as in the medical field where the focus is helping others more than enriching oneself. But under this heading of self-fulfillment I mean that many now see work as an important means of finding one's very meaning in the world. Probably most people have not spent a great deal of time working out a careful philosophy of work for themselves, but to judge from the way people often throw themselves into their work, their very life depends on it.

Of course, there is still the harsh necessity of earning a living. In our current circumstance of chronic underemployment this is no slight thing. Most people still need to work to live. It is not a luxury or a game. By and large Americans want to earn their own way; they certainly do not want to depend on the government in the form of unemployment insurance. This is such an important aspect of the American psyche that it actually threatens the very well-being of our whole society. When Americans are out of work they are unhappy, and they sometimes lapse into deep depression. So one should not disparage the making of a living. But it is still not as important as *meaningful work*.

Meaningful work may seem almost self-explanatory, but it may still merit some exploration. It is really the same issue of work that people find deeply satisfying in itself, no matter what other rewards it brings. It is also work in which people feel at home and completely involved. Granted, it takes time to work into some jobs, but the meaningful job is one in which I come to feel very alive and effective. There are jobs that are so engrossing that one does not watch the clock for quitting time to roll around. Probably the best examples of such jobs are those that involve an ideal with which the workers can identify. Of course, corporations typically try to convince their employees that their lives revolve around a certain brand of soap, etc. But other types of employment are virtually impossible to fulfill if one is not completely "sold" on the enterprise. For example, many non-profits do not pay their staff much, but they are really not working for the money anyway. They are committed to the cause.

The matter of meaningful work is not irrelevant to our monasteries. We have to face up to the fact that our monks and nuns are unhappy if they do not have meaningful work. Again, this is not just to keep them busy or to bring in enough money to put clothes on their backs. Most abbots and prioresses can find that kind of work for their people, but finding meaningful work may be much harder. To a great extent I think it is up to the individuals themselves. The day is probably over when the monk can expect the community to find him a meaningful job. Perhaps the first question would be: What do you really want to do? Is it compatible with monastic life? Does it bring in some money? Is it useful to the community? Yet it is still the hard fact that the community has to ask its members sometimes to take on work that does not seem very meaningful to the individual. With the grace of God it will become so as time goes on, but every monastery knows how much it depends on those who are willing to do sacrificial work.

Finally, something should probably be said about overwork. I think it is a very common malady in American monasteries. There are myriad reasons for this, and most of them have to do with our culture itself, not the specific situation of monastic life. Workaholism is very common in our culture, even rampant. Fifty years ago we often heard it said that we were on the threshold of a "leisure society" in which machines would do most of the unpleasant work and leave the average person with plenty of time on her hands for higher pursuits. Well, the future is here, but it isn't quite what we expected. At the beginning of the twenty-first century many people in our country work at two or three jobs, amounting to fifty or sixty hours a week. Often couples work twice that much.

Certainly not all these people *want* to work at that rate. Part of the problem is that too many jobs now do not pay a living wage and must be supplemented. Many jobs do not bring with them adequate benefits, which have to be found through additional work. There is also the issue of consumerism, which teaches people to want far more than they can afford; they find themselves slaving away to make the payments on all the superfluous machinery in the back yard. But plenty of people have to work harder than they should have to work just to keep body and soul together. The famous gap between the rich and the poor really means that the people with money have figured out a way to bilk the working class out of a just wage. If this sounds excessively Marxist, then so be it.

At any rate, overwork is also a problem in our monasteries. If many monks and nuns find their work fulfilling and fascinating, that can also become part of the problem, for it causes them to devote too much of their time and themselves to their work, no matter what it is. Often these same persons are very valuable to the institution, so no one wants to tell them they are working too hard. But for their own good they do need to hear this message. What does St. Benedict say? Well, he says nothing at all about overwork. But he does set up a horarium in RB 48 that attempts to create some kind of balance of the things he considers essential: prayer, reading, and work. I would be tempted to add a few things, like recreation, to this triumvirate, but no one element should be allowed to crowd out the rest.

It might be said that I am in fact undermining my own argument in this chapter by emphasizing Benedictine balance. In a sense that is true, since I have been claiming that we now take work more seriously than did Benedict or any of the old monks. There really does not seem to be a practical way to engage in serious work within the framework of the Benedictine horarium, at least if it is lived out to the letter. Yet it must also be noted that the rest of the monastic *trivium*, that is, prayer and reading, also can be hard work. At any rate, people only have so much energy and so much time.

But after all is said and done we have to stick to the principle that work is not the ultimate purpose of monastic life or of any other life. John Cassian (*Conference* 1) once made a nice distinction between the immediate purpose (*skopos*) and the ultimate purpose (*telos*) of the monastic life. He claimed that the *skopos* is "purity of heart" and the *telos* is heaven. Whatever "purity of heart" might be, it certainly cannot be translated into sheer work! No matter how satisfying our work might be, as monks and nuns we have a whole other dimension to our lives that has to be attended to. High achievement and production are usually rewarded in our society, and this also goes on in the monastery. Nonetheless, it is questionable whether that element will count much for a monk in the final judgment.

Chapter Seven   *Economics without Anxiety*

Economic Meltdown

One day in September of 2008 my niece's husband went to the airport to make a short business trip. When he saw the plunge of the stock market on the TV monitor he made a frantic phone call to his wife, saying that he was putting an immediate freeze on all spending in their household. My niece answered calmly that that was too bad, since she was just leaving for the grocery store. With no money for her to work with, his supper was going to be a little austere.

To understand the ridiculousness of this situation you have to know that this man is a very successful businessman. At age forty he is already a millionaire several times over. He owns a half-million-dollar house in a posh suburb and his family wants for nothing. He is extremely hard-driving and clever. I have no reason to think he is a crook; he comes by his money honestly. But he is obviously walking on thin ice where the least tremor sends him into a panic. Why all this anxiety?

In contrast, take my grandfather. He too was a successful businessman, but he had his ups and downs. In the 1920s and '30s he made and lost a couple of small fortunes. But according to my father, who was his son, you could never tell from his behavior whether he was rich or poor. He always remained calm and cheerful. He was totally lacking in the anxiety that stalks my nephew. Why the difference? I think we can see it from the analysis provided in a recent article by the eminent Old Testament scholar Walter Brueggemann.

According to Brueggemann the typical modern capitalist thinks the individual person is the primary unit of social reality. He feels he is dependent on no one, that is, he is an autonomous agent of his enterprises. He sees the world he functions in as "the market," a dog-eat-dog world where the fundamental rule is self-advancement. Moreover, since this is a world of scarcity his getting-ahead must happen at the expense of others. Sometimes he must play a little rough. In the words of Psalm 10:9-10 (RSV):

> His eyes stealthily watch for the hapless,
> He lurks in secret like a lion in his covert;
> He lurks that he may seize the poor,
> He seizes the poor when he draws him into his net.
> The hapless is crushed, sinks down, and falls by his might.
> He thinks in his heart, "God has forgotten,
> He has hidden his face, he will never see it."

But the Psalmist disagrees, and calls him a "fool" (10:4). He is a fool because in trying to live autonomously he has also lost his rootage in God. Without God's restraint he is also without his resource. And with his safety net gone he pays the heavy price of anxiety. In the language of the Stoics, he is an avaricious man, with the typical attitudes of that type. The avaricious person can never have enough material security. He is caught up in an endless rat race of achievement that produces bottomless anxiety. Here is a biting passage from Leviticus about such people:

> The sound of a driven leaf shall put them to flight, and they shall flee as one flees from the sword, and they shall fall when none pursues. They shall stumble over one another, as if to escape a sword, though none pursues; and you shall have no power to stand before your enemies. (Lev 26:36-37, RSV)

One of the byproducts of this bottomless dread is that the ruthless capitalist projects his anxiety on those who should not have the problem because they have no money. In other words, it serves the purposes of the greedy to convince the poor that they need to somehow shield themselves from disaster. This seems to be the explanation for how the politicians in recent decades have convinced the poor in the United States to vote against their own economic interests. Specifically they should give tax breaks to the rich, who will then protect them. We might call this the Preferential Option for the Rich.

Sometimes avarice takes particularly nasty forms, as with the current fiasco of subprime lending. The poor, or at least the lower middle class, were urged to buy things they really could not afford, such as lavish homes. They were given very favorable initial terms and were also told that they could not lose because the value of the home would continue to rise. As long as it did, they could borrow against it to pay their bills. But of course this was essentially a house of cards that had to collapse. Then they were foreclosed and the sharpies who talked them into this imprudent scheme in the first place were the only gainers.

I have to admit I do not understand all the ins and outs of these matters. I certainly don't deny that poor people deserve decent housing. But clearly a lot of the housing that has been going up recently is much more than "decent." Furthermore, none of this was exactly illegal. In fact, the government encouraged it by its various lending programs. But it was a basically flawed system that was hardly based on love for the poor. Its basis, rather, was ruthless greed, and sad to say it was the least rotten of the financial crimes committed by the current crop of economic cutthroats.

An Alternative Economics

Rather than pursue this melancholy account of our current practice of economics, let me turn to the Rule of St. Benedict, which has a rather different view of such matters. It must be said right away that Benedict is writing for people in a very different financial situation than the modern capitalist. He is writing for cenobitic monks with a vow of poverty. In practical terms this means that no one can become a Benedictine monk without completely divesting him- or herself of all worldly goods. From the minute of profession the monk owns nothing; it all belongs to the community. Still, I think Benedict's view of these things can also be helpful for anyone trying to live a decent Christian life.

Benedict has two little chapters expressly devoted to economic questions. RB 33–34 stand right next to each other and seem to have been created as a pair. They deal with the same subject, namely, the use of material goods, but they look at the issue from very different angles.

RB 33 is entitled "Whether monks should consider anything their own." Notice that it does not say "have" anything of their own. In fact, monks are not angelic beings. They need to use material things like food and clothes. The issue here, though, is how they should think about these things. In answer to that question Benedict is very blunt indeed: "This vice in particular must be torn up by the roots, that anyone should presume to give or receive anything without the abbot's permission, or consider anything personal property, absolutely nothing." To put it succinctly, private property is strictly forbidden to Benedictines.

Obviously this is hardly an ethic that can be applied to all humankind. When utopian revolutionaries such as the Russian Communists tried to put it into mass practice it produced something that horrified most Western people—or at least everybody but the kind of idealist philosophers Lenin and his gang read for their ideas. In the Bible the Acts of the Apostles seems to claim that the first Christians also pooled all their goods. I say "seems" because I doubt the text says that. At any rate, we know it caused massive upheaval in Russia, and eventually it proved untenable.

To return to RB 33, scholars have noticed that Benedict's remark about "tearing personal ownership up by the roots" is really a quotation from John Cassian. His *Institute* 7 is a treatise on avarice, and Cassian's take on this vice is much like what Brueggemann told us: the avaricious person can never have enough. The only antidote to this vice is to eradicate it altogether. It is something like the noxious weeds every farmer must deal with. Because they have such remarkable powers of regeneration they have to be completely destroyed.

Benedict is shrewd enough to know that the mere fact that his monks have made idealistic vows on entering the monastery does not mean they are no longer subject to the common human passions. As we said, a monk needs to use goods to maintain his body, but the constant danger, or at least possibility, is that he will slip back into the thought patterns of his social milieu. And in our society the prevailing "wisdom" in regard to goods and money is simple greed: get as much as you can as fast as you can.

Actually, Benedict does not have to rely on Cassian or Stoic doctrine to make this point. After all, the monk really lives in a different conceptual world than other people do. Hence Benedict's remark, which is the key verse of RB 33: "That is because they have neither their bodies nor their own wills at their own disposal." In other words, the monk has given away his whole life to God and the community. Why then would he want to renege on something as trivial as material goods? The argument is over-whelming, but of course it only applies to those with a vow of obedience.

To see how Benedict's thinking can have broader application we have to turn to the following chapter, RB 34, which is entitled "Whether all should receive necessities in equal measure." Given the tone of the previous chapter condemning all personal appropriation, we might think the answer here would be YES. But this is where Benedict might surprise us, because he says "As it is written: '*It was distributed to each one as any had need.*' (Acts 2:45, RSV)" This is in fact a verse from the Acts of the Apostles, which I just said does not teach pure communism. But the salient term here is *opus*, need.

Benedict makes it immediately clear here that he is not advocating some scheme of distributive justice in which everybody gets exactly the same rations. Instead, he is quite aware that everybody does not need exactly the same amount as his neighbor. That same point was made in Acts. They were not dealing with a utopian redistribution of resources there either. Rather, it was a question of practical charity. The community set out to try to make sure none of its members was suffering unnecessary need.

We should notice that the crucial point lies in their self-understanding as a group. Unlike the modern individualistic society in which people imagine they are somehow autonomous, the first Christians considered themselves a single body of believers. In the words of Paul, they believed they were the Body of Christ. The image of the body is very apropos here because it is not one of absolute equality. The body is a differentiated organism with different parts. They may not all be equally crucial, but they all need each other. Benedict then takes the further step of insisting that the only way for that body to be healthy is if all its members get what they need. To quote Benedict: "Then will all the members be at peace." Or to quote Pope Paul VI, "If you want peace, seek justice."

It should not be thought that Benedict dreamed this idea up on his own. In fact, even Paul was appealing to an earlier foundation. What was it? Brueggemann points to Deuteronomy 15, which teaches the radical economic ideal of the Jubilee. Every seven years all the accounts among the Israelites were to be wiped clean. All debts were to be forgiven and all land reverted to its ancestral family. And what was the justification for such a wildly utopian system? Simply this: "I freed you from the land of Egypt. Therefore, you shall not make slaves of your brothers and sisters."

You don't have to be a complete skeptic to wonder about such a system. For one thing, there is no hard evidence that it was ever practiced in Israel. And second, I am not sure how it could actually work, since it would seem to undercut all commerce as we know it. Who would want to buy a piece of land if he knew it would revert to the owner after seven years? Still, this is a view of economics that is so diametrically opposed to our own capitalist system that we should at least give it a moment's consideration. When an economy finds itself in the mess we are in, it should at least be humble enough to be willing to "think out of the box" for a few minutes.

We have to understand that the basis of such a revolutionary view of economics was not mercantile at all, but social. The basis for this approach was the conviction of the Jews that they were a *covenantal community*. They had been accepted into the loving arms of God by his mercy. They did not just rely on themselves but were operating with a divine "safety net" beneath them. Hence there was no reason for anxiety. Indeed, anxiety might be seen as sin since it means lack of trust in God. The corollary of this covenant with God is fraternity with the rest of the Jews, who were in the same covenant. This is really the basis of the ethics of the Jewish Bible.

As we have seen, one of the immense advantages of this kind of covenantal existence was the peace of mind it gave. But it also brought with it the corresponding duty to treat one another as brothers and sisters. In place of anxiety and the greedy economic war of all against all, the proper response to God's loving mercy was and is gratitude. And that must take the practical reflex form of generosity. It should also be mentioned that covenant faith also included the conviction of God's abundance. Instead of the economics of scarcity that seems to drive modern people, the good Jew believed that if you treated others generously there would be plenty left over.

To return to Benedict's chapter 34, it might be pointed out that it is really not as naïve as it might seem to be. In fact, it includes a short discussion of the spiritual problem of envy. Benedict knows full well that people are prone to look beyond their own needs and be controlled by their wants. Therefore he warns the monk who needs very little not to begrudge the monk who needs, and gets, much more. Here are his words: "So the one who needs less should thank God and not be sad. And whoever needs more should be humble about his weaknesses and not gloat over the mercy shown him" (RB 34.3-4).

This is a very astute passage, but again it is not original. Benedict is in fact condensing a large discussion from the Rule of Augustine, where the great North African monastic writer tries to find a way for the rich and the peasants to live together in community. It is doubtful that the economic background of Benedict's monks was quite so diverse as this, but he knows he must deal with the same problem of envy. And so he gives us the stunning maxim that the one who needs the least is the strongest. Now I would submit that in our consumerist culture this is rank heresy!

Perhaps you remember that right after the 9/11 disaster the President urged us all to go out shopping. Now I really don't know what he thought he would accomplish by that piece of advice. Maybe he just wanted to preserve us from too much anxiety and grief. But whatever it was, his remark was quite revealing of our national and cultural malaise. Of course, Bush was not the only one who took this approach. The British Government now has posters up showing a stern fellow with a handlebar mustache pointing at the onlooker and shouting: "Shop, Damn You, Shop!" This looks like bravado, but Benedict would say this is a sign of pitiful weakness.

I realize I might seem like an insufferable crank because in fact I do not have much of a stake in the present economic crisis. As someone said about the pope and sexual morality: "He no play-a da game, he no make-a da rules." I am not entirely cynical about capitalism, and I think I am well enough informed to know that a capitalist system does indeed need people to spend their money. As Churchill said about democracy, it might be a lousy system but it is by far the best one we have. The same goes for capitalism.

Still, it is a little hard to see how this same ethic of frantic consumption is not also at odds with that other nagging problem, namely, the state of the environment. I am not at all clear how we can continue consuming at the present rate and still hope to stave off the impending environmental disaster. After all, it is the same factories that produce our lavish lifestyle that are poisoning the air we must breathe. Without wading into this particular morass, let me finish by insisting that we will make no progress on either of these problems until we shift our thinking back to some form of covenantal community.

Chapter Eight

Food and Drink

Rule of Benedict

A glance at the index of Benedict's Rule shows that he was quite concerned with the monastic table. This in itself should not be surprising, since thoughtful people have always been careful what they eat and when they eat it. The traditional religions of the world spend a great deal of time thinking about food and fasting. Moreover, many people in our own time are also very concerned about their diet, though often for different reasons than formerly.

St. Benedict has two whole chapters on food plus several more on drink, table-waiting, and reading during meals. When we read RB 39 (On the Quantity of Food) and RB 41 (On the Times for Meals) we might get the impression that Benedict demands a good deal of discipline in these matters. This is quite true, but it is important to notice the precise form this asceticism takes in the Holy Rule. It is, for example, somewhat different from the traditional Catholic approach to fasting and abstinence. The church requires that its members abstain from meat on some days, and in addition they are sometimes bound to maintain a fast as well. For the church a "fast day" is essentially one on which we eat only one full meal. This main meal may occur at any time and it may be accompanied by one or two minor meals, but these latter may not amount to a main meal, giving two full meals for the day. This regime is still in place, but the number of fast days is now reduced to just two: Ash Wednesday and

Good Friday. The important thing to note here is that Catholic fasting is a question of *quantity*.

That is not exactly the case with St. Benedict. In RB 39 he stresses that monks should eat moderately, avoiding gluttony (39.8). In itself that is not a regime of asceticism but of moderation. This still leaves the question of what Benedict considers a moderate amount of food, and he spells this out quite clearly: a pound weight of bread and some variety of cooked food to accommodate different tastes. Overall one does not get the impression that Benedict is aiming at any extreme level of discipline in regard to quantity in food.

To better understand his thinking on the subject we also have to look at RB 41, where he discusses the times for meals. There he makes it clear that the main meal should normally take place at 3 p.m. (*nonam*). To our modern way of thinking that is quite late in the day to break one's fast. Benedict also seems to feel it is a long time to wait for food, so he allows the aged and children to eat earlier (RB 37). He allows the whole community to eat at noon during the festal Easter season (Easter to Pentecost), and when they do he wants them to leave some food aside for a lighter evening meal. On the other hand, the time for the single meal during Lent is deferred until evening.

Apart from these details the thing to notice is that for Benedict the culinary issue is not how much, but when. He says nothing about the amount of food to be taken at the main meal; he is just focused on when it should occur. This is a distinction monks need to keep in mind since it differs from the discipline of the main church. And those of us who lived during the old regime (before, say, 1970) may remember that we also had "monastic fast days" on Fridays. We always thought those days meant less food, not later food.

In regard to Benedict's horarium for meals we find the same attitude as for the amount of food. He is not at all rigid about making exceptions to his general pattern. Thus during the summer season after Pentecost he still allows for times when there will be a meal at noon and another lesser one in the evening. He says this practice should be allowed when the work load is heavy and/or there is excessive summer heat. This last point is somewhat puzzling, since many people feel the need for less food, not more, when it is hot. At any rate, Benedict urges the abbot to keep a sharp eye out for those situations when people seem to need to eat earlier and perhaps eat more (RB 41.4).

When we are talking about Benedict's moderation in regard to food we should not press this point too hard. By no stretch of the imagination is he *lax* in these matters! For example, everything he says about the food schedule implies that one does *not* eat between meals. As a matter of fact such undisciplined eating was strictly forbidden in all the ancient monastic Rules (see the Pachomian *Praecepta* 71 and 73), and it is clear that Benedict follows the trodden path in this matter. Otherwise why would he go out of his way to offer the table waiters (RB 35) and the table reader (RB 38) a bit of refreshment before they must serve the community?

It is also interesting to compare Benedict with the Rule of the Master in matters of food. When we do so we are in for a surprise. Given the general pattern of Benedict softening the usually harsher RM, we find that in questions of eating it is just the opposite: Benedict is less generous than the Master—or at least we can say he chooses to omit a food discussion that seems quite important to the Master. In RM 26.11-12 we read that the abbot may add some sweets to the diet on feast days. The Master also wants plenty of special wine at those meals. With Benedict there *are* no feast days!—or at least he does not mention them.

This silence about feasting does not mean that Benedict is mean-spirited or puritanical regarding food. Rather, he should be labeled *realistic.* When it comes to food his main principle is: people need enough food to maintain their health and also to do their work. It is quite clear that Benedict respects this axiom and continually reverts back to it in his various discussions of food. For Benedict there is no question of reversing the principle that food must serve life, and especially community life. He does not seem inclined to bend the common life to accommodate a certain level of asceticism in regard to food.

Again in this he is at odds with the Master. Although we have just pointed out his provision for feasting, it has to be added that for the Master the ordinary level of eating is *more ascetical* than for Benedict. How do we know this? We do not learn it from his main treatise on food (RM 26–28) but rather from a little chapter on farm work for monks (RM 86). In short, he's agin' it. Indeed, he says quite explicitly that monks should not be engaged in heavy field work because that will make it impossible for them to fast. They should not even manage farms! But Benedict feels differently about such things. In RB 48.7-9 he tells the monks that if necessity requires that they bring in the crop they should not waste time feeling sorry for themselves, but get to work. It seems to me that such a legislator is not going to withhold sufficient food from his workers. And field work requires a lot of food.

Indeed, it is hard to see how Benedict's monks could have gone without some kind of breakfast. When we remember that they rose at about 2 a.m. and spent hours in church before going out to work at about 6 a.m. it becomes almost mandatory that they would have eaten something along the way. It is all fine and good for intellectuals to talk about fasting as a good way to maintain a clear head (see the discussion of De Vogüé below). Manual labor requires more than a clear head. It requires physical energy, and that does not come from anything but sufficient food. Since Benedict always seems quite alert to the needs of workers it is hard to see how he could not know this.

Contemporary Point of View

At this point we have spent enough time looking at the ancient monastic approach to meals to know that it was at considerable variance with our own. In order to see this all we need to do is to ask a very practical question. Granting that a person only eats one main meal a day, what would that meal look like? Especially, if one were to take a fundamentalist angle on the question and not eat anything before, say, mid-afternoon, we can say that one would have to have a very big meal indeed! If this single meal is to provide all one's nourishment for the day and night, such a meal would have to encompass all that one would normally eat in three meals.

Now of course there is great variety in dietary needs among persons. Some people normally feel little hunger in the morning and thus wait till later in the day to do their eating. Others (including the present writer) have a hard time facing the day and its tasks without a substantial meal in the early morning. Without claiming that one or the other is to be preferred, we should just note here that there are simply different gifts with different people. Benedict himself recognizes this often enough, and in regard to food he provides for a couple of cooked dishes so "one who cannot eat one dish may be able to eat the other" (RB 39.2).

But what about other traditions? Nowadays we are especially aware of Islam, and some of us are even conversant with Islamic customs. One of the most important of their religious observances is Ramadan, which is the yearly month of fasting. In practical terms the observant Muslim may not eat or drink *anything* from sunrise to sunset. This is no joke in the hot countries where Islam typically flourishes. But it should be added that Islam says nothing about how much people may eat and drink while it is dark. And we know that for many Muslims Ramadan is a month of nightly feasting, not fasting. Still, the salient point here is simply that, like Benedict, Islam sees fasting largely as a question of timing, not quantity.

Or take another faith tradition, namely, Buddhist monasticism. I have seen it written that observant Buddhist monks do all their daily eating *before* noon. When I found myself part of a week of dialogue with these people some years ago I learned that they take this literally: lunch had to be finished by noon. I can attest that these monks did not skimp on the quantity of that meal, and they also ate a good breakfast. But they ate no supper at all. At any rate, here we have a perfect antithesis: Benedictine monks are not supposed to eat *before* noon, and Buddhist monks are not supposed to eat *after* noon! Which is the road to true spiritual fulfillment?

To return to the practical matter of the Benedictine monk eating one huge meal late in the day, it is hard to imagine anything so contrary to present-day medical wisdom in matters of food. When I contracted a serious liver ailment in recent years my gastroenterologist had very little to say to me regarding diet. But one thing he did say: Do not eat for two hours before you go to bed for the night! Someone who lives a normal Western schedule will have no trouble observing that, since most of us eat our evening meal about 6 or 7 p.m. and retire about 10 or 11 p.m. But someone following the Rule of Benedict to the letter will find herself having to retire on a full stomach, especially during Lent.

This kind of late eating is by no means just a peculiarity with the ancient monks. Rather, it is standard Mediterranean practice to this day. One of the surprises the American tourist encounters in a place like Rome is that you can hardly find a restaurant willing to serve you before 8 p.m.! And it gets worse when you go to Madrid. There people take their evening meal about 9:30 p.m., and to judge from the empty streets they go directly to bed. It is also said that fancy dinner parties in South America are often scheduled for 10 p.m. But if you are foolish enough to come on time you will find yourself cooling your heels until about midnight, when the food is finally served.

How much of Benedict's wisdom on fasting can be attributed to his Mediterranean context? No doubt some of it. Certainly those of us who live in very cold climates have to take some of his strictures about not eating meat with a grain of salt, or at least we have to be realistic enough to know that one needs a certain amount of protein to function in harsh climates, and especially to work out of doors. Of course, many people now avoid red meat for hygienic, not ascetic, reasons. But all of us have to come to terms with what our bodies actually need in the concrete circumstances in which we find ourselves.

I keep returning to that one huge meal Benedict seems to prefer for his monks. How can this be a good thing? We know, for example, that when people have stomach problems, and especially when they have surgery, they have to avoid large meals. Indeed, many people are now required for medical reasons to eat smaller, more frequent meals. Clearly they cannot follow Benedict's strict regime either. On the other hand, the constant snacking modern people seem prone to is not a good thing. Indeed, dieticians now suggest that such nibbling is directly connected with the obesity that has become almost epidemic in our society.

One monastic scholar who has taken a great interest in Benedict's dietary regime is Adalbert de Vogüé. Since he is arguably the greatest RB expert of modern times one is well advised to take seriously whatever he says about the Rule. One of his bedrock principles is his literalistic approach to food. Vogüé eats one big meal a day, usually in the late afternoon. Not only that, he has written a book on the subject entitled *To Love Fasting* (St. Bede's Press, 1994). Realizing that many, perhaps most people are going to find his call for literal observance of Benedict's eating rules somewhat outlandish, Vogüé tells us to restrain our skepticism and reserve judgment until we have actually tried it.

This is not an argument one can refute on abstract grounds. All we can say is that if it "works" for Vogüé, then more power to him. But we can also add that even if such a program does suit one's constitution, that does not mean it is particularly feasible for life in our present society. If one wishes to eat with other people, this cannot always be deferred to late afternoon or evening. And it is also difficult to eat with other people if you need to work through a vast amount of food, as is the case if you eat but once a day. But of course Vogüé does not run into these problems because he lives as a hermit. He does not have to take other people into account in these matters.

But taking other people into account as regards food is actually one of St. Benedict's main concerns. For example, Benedict's inspiring chapter 35 on the table servers (waiters) begins with the starkly powerful aphorism: "The brothers should serve one another." Of course that does not only apply to meals, but it does seem to have special application in that case. It should also make us think a bit about our modern practice of cafeteria service. Granted, somebody must prepare the food on the line so that others may pick it up for themselves. Yet nothing can really replace the basic human practice of table service in which waiters directly supply the diners and care for their basic needs. If we find it inconvenient nowadays to wait on tables, we might reflect that all true service comes at the expense of self-accommodation.

But mutual service at table can take other shapes than formal table-waiting. Probably more basic is the simple act of the diners caring for one another during the meal. In fact, Benedict seems to have thought a lot about this himself. In his chapter 38 on the weekly reader at table he makes the following comment: "As they eat and drink, the brothers should serve the needs of one another so that no one has need for anything." He follows this by the bewildering verse: "If it is necessary, however, one should make his request by some audible signal rather than by voice." In fact, monks traditionally signaled their needs by silent sign language, not audibly. But we cannot settle this exegetical problem in an essay like this.

Yet we need to complete our remarks on Vogüé's book before we finish here. In recent years his little book was displayed in the bookstore of one of our American monasteries. One day the local abbot received a visit from a couple of medical doctors who happened to be making a retreat at the abbey. They advised the abbot to take Vogüé's book out of the bookstore since they felt it promotes unhealthy dietary practices. It is not reported whether the abbot heeded their advice. Since he himself was a medical doctor he may have decided they were wrong. But the incident is still worth thinking about, for it shows clearly the disjunction that can exist between an ancient monastic practice and modern medical thinking.

On this same line, the issue of hydration may be even more problematic. Although Benedict says very little about liquid as such, he does allow the table reader a drink of diluted wine before the meal: "The brother who is the weekly reader should receive some diluted wine before he reads. This is because of the Holy Communion and because he may find it difficult to endure the fast." From this text it looks like Benedict is treating this wine as nourishment, but his monks apparently did not have easy access to good drinking water. And it is quite likely that their ascetical ideology discouraged them from drinking more water than absolutely necessary.

This same attitude can be seen in one of the many practical stipulations in the Pachomian Rule:

> If the brothers who are sent out on business or are staying far away eat outside the monastery, the weekly server who accompanies them shall give them food but without making cooked dishes, and he shall himself distribute water as is done in the monastery. No one may get up to draw or drink water. (*Praecepta* 64)

This is but one instance of the Pachomian principle that the monk is *not to take care of himself*, but should submit to the ministrations of a confrère. It also shows that a simple thing like a drink of water was not taken for granted. For one thing, water was scarce, and clean drinking water was hard come by even on the banks of the Nile where the Pachomian monks dwelt. But when we remember what a torrid climate they lived in it can seem almost unbelievable that they did not have free access to water. Surely there was an ascetical idea that indiscriminate drinking of any kind was bad for one's spiritual discipline.

This point of view is even clearer in the writings of John Cassian, who comes a little later than Pachomius but earlier than Benedict. In one of his remarkable treatises on chastity (*Conferences* 12.9-11) he takes up the problem of nocturnal emission for males. He says one of the ways to counteract it is to drink less before going to bed. Of course, anybody who has arrived at a mature age knows as much, but we think of the matter in practical terms of trips to the bathroom. Cassian, however, is thinking in strictly ascetical terms, and he recommends a restricted intake of water to avoid erection and pollution. But apart from this remarkably frank approach to a delicate subject we have to say it does seem highly dubious to our present way of thinking, for if there is one piece of advice that can be counted on from the doctors it is this: "drink plenty of water." It is not just because we live in an arid climate, because most of us do not. The plain fact is that the physical organism needs to be adequately hydrated to function properly. For one thing, the various secretions of the glands need to be kept sufficiently moist to maintain their flow. People with deadly ailments such as pancreatic disfunction know how crucial this can be. But beyond that, dehydration in general is a serious problem, and partly because it is so insidious. Dehydration creeps up on us, and if we don't know the warning signs it can lay us low before we know it. The only sensible means of keeping it at bay is simply to drink water, and keep on drinking water.

Parenthetically, older Catholics also remember that the eucharistic fasting rules prohibited the drinking of water after midnight for morning Mass. Nobody seemed to consider this a health issue at the time, but it is almost certain that it would not be acceptable today.

At any rate, here is a rather dramatic example of how modern medicine and hygiene take a different view from the ancient monastic approach to eating and drinking. For them it was essentially an ascetic question, and we still cannot deny it is that. Eating and drinking is a moral issue and one that is certainly not disconnected from a healthy spiritual life. But it is not just a spiritual question. There are ways to eat and drink that are conducive to promoting good health and other practices that are not. We cannot look just to the old monks for advice on these matters. We also have to listen to our doctors.

Chapter Nine   *Mobility and Stability*

Mobility

When we are discussing the interface between contemporary culture and the ancient Benedictine Rule it is obvious that mobility is about "us" and stability about "them," that is, the old monks. And yet in the reflections that follow it will emerge that we are not completely mobile and they were not completely stable. Allow me to mull over the present situation through the lens of some personal family history.

Recently our family had a reunion of sorts that was remarkable in its makeup. To wit: there were twenty-five people from eight states! Without naming those eight states I can just say that the whole thing involved a great deal of going to and coming from airports, coordinating schedules, and so forth. Many of us hadn't seen each other for years, so it was one of those affairs that resembles a class reunion.

The occasion was the death of our maiden aunt in Los Angeles, where she had lived for the last twenty-five years. Like many people in California my aunt had no relatives living within a hundred miles, but my sister visited her often from Minneapolis and gradually took over her affairs as she declined. One day my sister did not receive her regular phone call from the old lady, and she asked our cousin in San Diego to please drive up to Los Angeles and check on Aunt Shirley. When she broke into the house she found the poor old woman unconscious on the bathroom floor, where she had been for God knows how long. Happily, she did not die alone.

Then the family met for a memorial service in Minneapolis some months later. Since I am the clergyman in the family I was asked to say Mass for the occasion. Fair enough, but I wondered how many of the people who would be present were actually Catholics any more. I had reason to suspect that most of them were not, and sure enough there were few communions. Nevertheless, Aunt Shirley was a pious Catholic and we all knew she would want to be remembered at a Mass. The service was but another sign that the family is simply falling apart at the seams. Mobility has done us in.

What a contrast to fifty years ago! We were a typical 1950s provincial clan with a patriarch, imperial aunts, and so forth. The world was simple. It was extremely stable. My mother and her friends were a remarkable example of this era. When they were in high school in the 1920s they joined the Pen Pals, which was a national organization in which people actually wrote letters to each other. They wrote to people in faraway places, people they had never met in person, so at one point my Mom and some friends took a long jaunt to places like Cleveland and Buffalo to meet their Pen Pals face to face.

As you might expect, these girls soon stopped writing letters. As young wives and mothers they were far too busy. But they did not stop meeting on the local level. Once a month they gathered at somebody's house for a social evening. There was nothing so unusual about that since they were all Catholics from St. Paul, mostly of German-American descent. What was unusual, what was astounding, was that they never broke up! That is, they met regularly for over fifty years. In fact, the only thing that could break up that rock-solid group of friends was death itself.

When I look back on the Pen Pals they seem like the absolute epitome of stability. As I remember them, though I'm sure I don't know all the facts, they never changed. They never moved out of the Twin Cities, they never lapsed in their Catholicism, they never got divorced. Now, I am sure there must have been some changes in their membership. I know one of my aunts joined the group after many years, and some of them drifted away. But still, it was almost as if the Pen Pals were in a bubble where time stood still. I don't want to present this as some kind of ideal. I am sure there were negative aspects to it. But it was at the extreme other end of the spectrum from where our family is today.

Another example of this same phenomenon was my father's approach to employment. He worked for Pittsburgh Plate Glass for forty years as an accountant. It seemed to us that he worked hard and had a responsible position, but he never made any real money. Why? Because Pittsburgh wanted him to move to different cities and he refused. So he never advanced in the corporate structure.

Why did he refuse to budge? I think it was because of my mother. She had so many good friends and connections in the Twin Cities that she wasn't about to pull up stakes. Whether this was okay with my father I don't know. He was too busy making a living to have time for friends. Not my mother! Of course, she never worked full time out of the home, but it was clear that she had many cultural and social connections that were important to her. For example, she played violin in an amateur orchestra that used to provide Sunday afternoon concerts in the local orphanages and prisons. I remember this because I played the piano during intermissions. I was about six years old.

Now my sister says that she wishes our parents had not decided to forego corporate advancement. How did they expect to make any money? It was true that we did not have any. They bought a house for $13,000 in 1950 and it took them maybe fifteen years to pay it off. But I am profoundly grateful to my parents for *not* moving around the country. To stay put meant I had the luxury of living with our extended family and going to the same parochial school for seven years. Minneapolis was, and always will be, my *home town*. When I go there, infrequently, I feel profoundly at home. I think this stability is an essential part of my psyche.

Eventually, of course, the family started breaking up. People moved to places like Tucson, San Diego, and Los Angeles. They said they were sick and tired of scraping the ice off the windshield in the morning and driving on dangerous roads. They also were glad to be clear of the heavy state taxes in Minnesota. But they were not so happy with the poor social services in the Sun Belt, and they sometimes complained about the shiftless Hispanics who did their yard work. I had to bite my tongue when I listened to that kind of talk.

Stability

St. Benedict is famous for his emphasis on stability. Indeed, it is one of the three promises he requires from the monk upon his acceptance into the community (RB 58.9, 17). Yet is not perfectly clear what Benedict means by the term stability. In itself the term *stabilitas* refers to the maintenance of place, but it could also have a moral and spiritual meaning having to do with perseverance in one's pursuit of holiness. The Benedictines are the only Order that promises stability, but all religious Orders pursue lifelong holiness. Benedictines also promise obedience and a monastic manner of life, and they implicitly promise chastity and poverty as well. So it would not be right to see stability as the quintessential Benedictine vow. Still, it must be important, since Benedict mentions it many times.

The first appearance of stability in the Rule occurs in the first chapter. Actually, the reference here is negative since Benedict rails against the "gyrovagues," monks who are notoriously *unstable*. Perhaps they were something like the people we still meet today who seem to have visited every monastic guestroom in the country. But the ancient gyrovagues claimed they were real monks. Just because they had no ties to any particular monastery didn't disqualify them, at least in their own eyes.

Benedict's rather bitter complaints about the gyrovagues should be seen in context. There were in fact good monks in his time who *purposely* left their homelands and wandered for penance. The Irish monks of the early Middle Ages were the best-known example of this. They weren't wasting their time: they re-evangelized Western Europe at a time when Catholicism there was in a somewhat decadent state. But it seems that Benedict distrusted the whole idea of monastic pilgrimage. In his eyes it was just an excuse for living outside the constraints of monastic obedience, always a dangerous fantasy for communal monks.

At any rate, Benedict loved stability so much that at one point he did not hesitate to say this: "The workshop where we should work hard at all these things is the monastic enclosure and stability in the community" (RB 4.78). Strictly speaking this sentence is an anomaly since it is not logical to call stability in the community a workshop. But if we allow Benedict some latitude of expression we get his point. He is saying that a stable life in a monastic community is a good environment in which to work at growth in the monastic virtues. And we might draw the negative corollary that it is hard to achieve spiritual growth apart from a stable community of some sort.

This same kind of thinking was applied by the Desert Fathers to the question of movement by the hermits. There was a saying among them that went like this: "Take care of your cell and your cell will take care of you." The cell was the hermitage, and the point was that you had to stay home to do any serious soul work. Although those desert cells might not have been quite as austere as we imagine them, nevertheless it was assumed that the most important thing that went on there was solitary prayer. Certainly the monks had to go out for various necessities, but they were warned that aimless wandering about was a sure way to forfeit any possibility of spiritual progress.

In Benedict's chapter on the training of a novice we read the following revealing passage:

> If he promises to persevere in his stability, after a period of two months let this Rule be read straight through to him. Then tell him: Here is the law

you wish to serve under. If you can keep it, come in. If not, you are free to leave. If he is still determined, he should be taken back to the novice quarters and again tested in all patience. And after a period of six months let the Rule be read to him so he knows what he is getting into. If he still holds his ground, the Rule should be read to him again after four months. (RB 58.9-13)

It isn't too clear why the Rule was read so many times to the novice and at precisely these intervals. What is crucial in this passage is whether the novice is "holding his ground." That, after all, is the root meaning of stability: to stand firm. Indeed, that seems to be the point of the vow of stability: to hold one's ground. In the face of what? The implication is that there are all kinds of forces threatening to overturn the novice in his determination to join the monastic brotherhood.

To be quite frank, this whole question of monastic rootedness has become a peculiar problem for contemporary persons. For many of us final commitment, far from being a satisfying prospect, appears to be a terrifying threat. To judge from the way some young monks and nuns are putting off final vows from year to year it looks as if they are afraid of being trapped. Perhaps they feel they are so personally fragile that they cannot risk this kind of ultimate commitment. Marriage makes the same requirements, but then marriage isn't exactly prospering either. So stability is a huge modern issue.

Actually, the question of firmness in one's commitment has been with us throughout Christian history. We find it so from the very beginning in the early persecutions: when the Roman government began threatening Christians with death if they refused to pay the emperor divine homage some "stood their ground" and others capitulated. Indeed, the New Testament has a special word for holding your ground in faithfulness to Jesus Christ to the end: *hypomonē*. And we all remember the saying: "She who perseveres till the end will be saved" (see Matt 10:22).

When we compare monastic stability with the faithfulness of the early martyrs we are far from the mere issue of not leaving the enclosure. But throughout this discussion we have seen that stability has this inherent ambiguity: it can refer to places or persons. In fact, the phrase "stability in the community" (RB 4.78) refers to persons, not places. Nowadays most commentators on the Rule of Benedict recognize that this is the deepest level of cenobitic stability. We commit ourselves to a given community of people; whether we always live among them is not as important as if we are devoted to them as our primary community. There have been many monks who have been assigned by obedience to live apart from the group for long periods of time with no apparent loss of their attachment to the community.

Nevertheless, Benedict does put a good deal of emphasis on stability of place, and it is important that we examine a couple more texts to take full account of this. Here is a famous passage:

> If possible, the monastery should be built so that all necessities such as water, mill and garden are contained within the walls so they can practice the various crafts there. That way it will not be necessary for the monks to venture outside, for that is certainly not beneficial to their souls. (RB 66.6-7)

When I first came to the monastery where I am still a member there was some semblance of Benedict's ideal of self-sufficiency. For example, the monks generated their own electric power. They ate a simple diet that featured a good deal of canned produce from their kitchen garden. The community had only a couple of cars and there was very little use of them. People still talked as if they were proud to be so self-sufficient.

Sixty years later all that is a distant memory. Now we live in a very different world. For example, we used to subsist on the water from our own well, which we drank untreated. Nowadays we drink water from a regional pipeline, water that is chlorinated and treated according to state specifications. Years ago when the monks built something they did the work themselves, and it was rather rough and ready. Now we generally bring in professional contractors; now everything must be "up to code." That is the kind of world we now live in. But Benedict has more to say about stability of place in the next chapter:

> Brothers who are about to set out on a journey should commend themselves to the prayers of all the brethren and the abbot. A remembrance of all the absent members must always be made at the final prayer of the Divine Office. But when the brothers come back from a journey, they should return that very day for all the canonical hours. And while the Work of God is coming to an end, they should prostrate on the floor of the chapel. They must ask all to pray for them on account of their faults, for they may have been surprised by the sight of wicked things or the sound of harmful words. And no one should presume to tell anyone else what he has seen or heard outside the monastery, for that causes great harm. (RB 67.1-5)

From this passage it is obvious that the monks did not in fact stay at home all the time. They had to make journeys, and some of them were quite long. For example, we know that monks were sometimes sent with death notices from abbey to abbey. As they went they would collect more notices, and these journeys could take up to a year. That they could be quite burdensome comes out clearly in a passage from the Rule of the Master, which threatens with punishment any monk who *refuses* to make a business trip enjoined on him by monastic obedience!

In the Middle Ages, not too long after the time of Benedict, monasteries began to accumulate property at some distance from the monastery. These farms, which were called granges, usually were managed by the lay brothers. They tried to make it to the abbey for Sunday Mass, but by and large they were on their own. No more talk about it "not being good for their souls." It was good for the monastic treasury, so it was permitted. Most of this property was donated to the monks; they did not purchase it. But it very often caused the monastery legal troubles, and some of the abbots spent much of their time in court.

Benedict himself did not envisage such a thing. Rather, he tried to keep his monks home as much as possible for their own spiritual good. It is clear from this passage that Benedict felt the surrounding society posed a good deal of danger to the soul of the monk. The idea that they were not to talk about what they had seen and heard certainly says a lot. Benedict felt that the monastic enclosure was to function as a *cordon sanitaire* to shield the monks from the harmful influences of the secular world.

I can think of two things to say about this matter, considering the circumstances in which we now find ourselves. First, if it ever was possible to really enclose a monastic community, it no longer is so. You can build all the walls you want, but if the monks want to know what is going on in the world they will find out. Obviously the mass media are the way most people connect with the world, and monks are no different. But there are different levels of engagement. One can watch the news once a week or one can follow it all day long on one's personal computer. Generally speaking it is folly to try to enclose people who do not wish to be enclosed.

Yet even this begs another question: is it good for the monk's soul to be *unaware* of what is going on in the world? Granted, there is very much out there that is utterly banal and useless, the kind of stuff nobody needs to know about the world. This is often what the popular news media is about. But there is a lot more out there that is very important, and also important for monks to know. I can see absolutely no virtue in a monk or a monastic community remaining ignorant of the various issues of social justice in the region and the world.

Years ago we used to hear about communities in which the abbot alone would read the papers. He then would inform the monks of the news and also provide them with a proper interpretation. I suppose this was not exactly an absurd situation but it certainly didn't give the monks much credit for maturity and discernment. Granted, when people are given free access to the media some of them will probably abuse it. I know a few monks who gravitate to the worst kind of political viewpoint (not my own!). There is no help for this malady that I know of. But the day is gone when we can spare monks from knowing about the troubles of the world.

So it would seem that Benedict's ideas about stability operate on at least two levels. Since our present world is so very different from the sixth century it is doubtful that we can hold to his ideas about monastic enclosure in any kind of fundamentalist manner. But his theme of stability of the heart is a different matter. Rootedness in God and in the community is an abiding Benedictine value.

Chapter Ten

Monastic Garb

Vatican II on Religious Garb

One of the noticeable effects of Vatican II among religious was the change of clothing among the nuns. Many of them put aside their traditional habits entirely and simply began to dress like laywomen. This change did not come about abruptly nor was it done without a good deal of stressful conflict. Most of the nuns first adopted a modified habit, but within about five years after the council the majority of them took on "civvies." What caused this big shift? It was basically a response to a direct request of the council for a modification of the habit. *Perfectae Caritatis* 17 puts it plainly enough:

> Since they are signs of a consecrated life, religious habits should be simple and modest, at once poor and becoming. They should meet the requirements of health and be suited to the circumstances of time and place as well as to the services required by those who wear them. Habits of men and women which do not correspond to those norms are to be changed.

For our purposes here the salient item in this statement of the council is that it is addressed to *both* women and men religious. Yet it is a curious fact that most religious men, and especially most monks, have paid no attention to it. By and large the habits of Benedictine men throughout the world are exactly the same as they were in 1960, not to say 1560!

Of course it is hard to prove a negative, but we might at least venture a preliminary hunch as to why the men did nothing about this conciliar mandate. If you would consult the average monk he is probably happy enough to see that some of the more outlandish habits of the nuns have been jettisoned. But he sees this as essentially a feminine problem, not pertaining to him. After all, isn't the male Benedictine habit perfectly serviceable?

No, it is not. Or at least it does not meet the criteria set down by PC 17. First of all, it is not "simple." The typical habit comes in at least three pieces, namely, cassock, belt, and scapular. For feastday liturgies the monk in solemn vows wears an additional choir robe called a cuculla. All of this paraphernalia is so complex and difficult to put on and take off that disabled and feeble monks often cannot cope with it. Second, it is not particularly healthy. In hot, humid weather it becomes a sweaty prison chamber, and it is notoriously hard to keep clean. A black habit often must be drycleaned at considerable expense. It cannot be said that such garb is ordinary clothing for *any* modern time or place. It is simply medieval clothing. Finally, such a garment greatly restricts the kind of work the wearer can do. It is certainly not something to be worn around powerful machinery!

The fact is that the contemporary Benedictine habit is really not "clothing" at all, but a ceremonial gown, and that is the way most modern monks use it. They put it on for church and usually for meals, but when it comes to work they take it off. This means that the average monk gets in and out of his habit three or four times a day, but you rarely hear them complain about it. One gets used to such things and never thinks about them. This rather bizarre and irrational behavior is simply taken for granted.

One of the reasons "the habit" goes unchallenged is that it has been around so long. According to historians of the monastic habit it has remained basically unchanged since the Middle Ages! There are other ways of living that also have gone unmodified for centuries, but surely this is one of the oddest. What makes it almost unbelievable is that the clothing of other people, at least most people in the West, has been greatly modified during the same period. To put it as simply as possible, men have begun to wear pants and shirts instead of loose-fitting "dresses." And the same also goes for a lot of women in our time.

At this point someone with a sense of history might wonder what St. Benedict has to say about all this. Might it not be that modern monks are simply following his Rule to the letter? It would be nice to say that they are, but they are not. As a matter of fact, the present design and usage of the Benedict habit does not go back to St. Benedict at all. As we will see, it goes back a long way, but not to the source. Benedict himself had a lot to say about the clothing of his monks, but much of it is simply ignored by Benedictine monks throughout the world.

RB 55: Practical Arrangements for Clothing the Monks

As the subtitle indicates, this chapter is not exactly directed to the monk, nor does it tell him how to clothe himself. Rather, it is meant for the abbot as part of a larger discussion on his obligation to see that the monks' needs are met. RB 33 and RB 34 tell the monks to look to the abbot and the community for what they need. They are not to take care of themselves. The other side of the coin is that the dispossessed monk must then be properly taken care of. In regard to clothing, what does this entail?

Rather than first listing the items of clothing the monk should receive, as one finds in the Rule of the Master (RM 81), Benedict opens RB 55 with the rather surprising provision that the monks should receive clothes suitable to the "circumstances and the climate." This may seem an altogether unremarkable statement but it is actually quite significant in establishing the author's basic attitude toward clothing: it is essentially a practical matter. One might ask: what else might it be? In fact, there are many other possibilities. For example, two of the most famous monastic theoreticians, namely, Evagrius Ponticus and John Cassian, look on monastic garments as primarily symbolic. Thus in *Institute* 1 Cassian assigns a theological or spiritual meaning to every piece of the habit. Some of this allegorization seems quite farfetched to us today, but at least it shows that clothes are not only a practical matter.

At this point it is important to note that the clothes Benedict prescribes, namely, cowl, tunic, and scapular, were not what we would call a "monastic habit" at all, but rather the clothing of the ordinary people of the time. The tunic was simply the ancient form of underwear, which was also worn to sleep in. The cowl was some kind of cloak or shirt over the tunic, fastened with a belt or cincture, and the scapular was basically a work apron. It might be added that the cowl and scapular were usually not worn at the same time; it was either one or the other.

How can we claim that this ensemble of clothing was the same as what was worn by the average person in the sixth century? Simply from Benedict's remark that when the various pieces of the wardrobe become worn they should be given to the poor (RB 55.9). If these items were very different from what the poor normally wore they would not find them very useful as a gift or as alms. If the clothing of Benedict's monks was similar to that of the laity, was it possible to recognize a monk if you saw him in the street? Most likely it was, since all monks wished to be distinguished by some kind of symbol. Here is a quotation from St. Basil of Caesarea to that effect: "Let our clothing be common and the same for all alike. A mere glance should recognize a Christian. For the weak, a garment befitting a religious calling is like a leader; it also discourages the restless from unfaithful and disobedient behavior" (*Latin Rule* 11).

It should be admitted that this remark of Basil is really aimed at *all* Christians, whom he thought should live a different lifestyle than the local pagans. Elsewhere Basil, like Benedict in RB 55, says that the material for this clothing is not too important. Rather than worry about the color or the texture the monks should look for cloth that was easily available locally and not expensive. Of course that precludes almost all the material used in modern monastic habits, but we will let that go for now. Before we leave St. Basil we should perhaps point out that his Rule may be the main inspiration for RB 55. We suspect this might be the case because both Rules repeat the same leitmotif in regard to clothing, namely, *sufficit* (it is enough). In RB 55.4, 10, and 15 Benedict intones this unremarkable verb, which actually packs a great deal of meaning when examined a bit more closely. For his part Basil has the same triple usage in *Latin Rule 9*, which could be Benedict's source for RB 55.

What makes "enough" so significant? Simply the fact that it is very easy to violate basic frugality in regard to clothes, and especially ceremonial clothes. Anybody who has glanced at modern fashion magazines knows the lengths to which people will go to adorn themselves with sumptuous and sometimes outlandish clothes. The Catholic and Orthodox liturgies also tend to feature gorgeous ceremonial garments, which sometimes verge on the preposterous. But Basil and Benedict think monastic clothing should just be "enough."

To return to the standard clothes Benedict prescribes for his monks, we also notice that he arranges for special garments for travel, namely, better (probably newer) items and also pants. In doing this he seems to be conforming to the ordinary practice of travelers in his day. Pants for a traveler were especially appropriate if he was going on horseback. In Northern Europe, of course, they were necessary everywhere in the wintertime. As for "better garb" for travel, that was probably what most people wore who had to travel any distance—unless they were poor beggars. But the salient point here is that Benedict wants the clothing of monks to be appropriate for all kinds of situations. In that sense it is real *clothing* and not a ceremonial garment only fit for the liturgy.

Subsequent History

When we ask how Benedict's followers carried out his wishes in regard to clothing we have to admit that they were not very faithful to it. Monastic historians have long been aware that there was a distinct break in the Benedictine tradition after the destruction of Monte Cassino by the Lombards about 577. For at least a hundred years after that we have no solid evidence of monasteries in Italy, or anywhere else for that matter, adhering to the Rule of Benedict. When evidence of such influence does begin to peep through, the Rule is always used in addition to other Rules such as that of Columban. Therefore it should not surprise us that many practical aspects of the RB underwent early modification.

The earliest extensive evidence we have of the implementation of the Rule in regard to clothing comes with the provisions of the Synod of Aachen in 817. For that momentous chapter meeting for the abbots of the whole Carolingian Empire, Benedict of Aniane produced a rather detailed list of the items of clothing a good monk ought to have and use. Since Benedict of Aniane was a rather stern and rigorous monastic reformer we might expect that he would take a hard line on monastic clothing. Not at all! Instead we find a much expanded list (Aachen Decrees XX) that includes all kinds of items Benedict himself probably would have found excessive. For example, each monk is to be equipped with a fur coat for winter, and he is to receive two or three sets of the other pieces as well.

What could be the motivation of this surprising liberalization of monastic clothing by Benedict of Aniane? Probably it was a simple matter of climate. To put it plainly, it is a lot colder in northern France than in southern Italy in winter. By and large there is no way a person could keep soul and body together in Germany wearing just Benedict's tunic and scapular. Most likely Benedict of Aniane was simply adhering to Benedict's basic dictum that "circumstances and climate" must be taken into consideration. In that sense he was true to the Rule. Whenever monks have forgotten this utterly realistic principle they have paid the price. For example, the customs of La Pierre-qui-Pire in France did not permit that a fire be used in the monastery. When those monks attempted to live out that precept in Oklahoma (U.S.A.) in the 1880s, half of them died of tuberculosis. I think Benedict would have shaken his head sadly.

After the Synod of Aachen the monastic life in Europe was nearly wiped out by barbarian invasions, but it soon revived in Cluny and in the so-called imperial monasteries of France and Germany. In regard to Cluny we know that these monks greatly expanded the liturgical emphasis Benedict of Aniane had already made in the Benedictine horarium. They spent endless hours in church every day. That being the case, it is not surprising that they paid a lot of attention to the ceremonial garments they wore for those liturgies. In particular they developed a distinctive type of cuculla in which the sleeves fell all the way to the floor. Such an outfit may look somewhat stylish, but it is altogether impractical. What to do with all that cloth?

The Cluniac customaries make elaborate arrangements but they cannot hide the fact that they are dealing with something essentially irrational.

To make things worse, Cluniacs were rather aggressive in spreading their hegemony and their customs throughout Europe. That meant they were quite ready to impose their strange cucullas on the monks in places like Germany where there was no such custom. Since the Cluniac takeover was rather "hostile" in some cases, that meant clothes could easily become a flash point in the controversy. In his remarkably polemical 1950 doctoral thesis on "Gorze and Cluny" the German monastic historian Kassius Hallinger reflected bitterly on the arrogance and aggression of the Cluniacs toward the imperial monasteries. It is significant that much of Hallinger's book is taken up with an analysis of different styles of monastic garb.

Whether the medieval monks cared as much about clothing styles as Hallinger did is perhaps questionable. What is certain, though, is that there had been a big change since RB 55. It is hard to imagine Benedict caring all that much about the length of the sleeves on the cucullas! He wants the garments to fit, but that is a long way from parsing every little shift in the cut and style of the clothes. Yet, as Hugh Feiss has recently remarked, the medieval monks were intent on establishing their distinct forms of monastic observance. For them clothing was very much a symbol of their distinct take on the monastic life itself. Clearly, it was *more* than just a *practical* matter!

One case in which this was very apparent was the Cistercian reform. When those monks wanted to separate themselves from the old Benedictine ways they made sure to change their garb. In this case the basic intent was simplification, and so they created plainer garments with fewer pleats, and so forth. But they also changed the basic *color* of the monastic tunic from black to white. This in itself was a blatant gesture and drew down on them the recriminations of people like Peter the Venerable, Abbot of Cluny. Actually, the Cistercians went to an off-white tunic because they began to wear undyed wool. In this way they controlled the whole process since they often had their own sheep. Thus they did not have to bear the considerable expense of having the cloth dyed.

Peter's insistence on *black* tunics should also be seen in its proper historical context. The color black, which has since become almost the trademark of the Benedictines (think: Black Monks) is actually not original at all. St. Benedict himself says nothing about it in RB 55; instead he says "they should not worry about the color." And from what we can tell, the early medieval monks did not worry about it. We have many paintings of monks from the period around 900 AD and few of them are wearing a stitch of black. Whether it was because black was an expensive color to dye or whether they found it lugubrious I don't know. But it was only the Council of Vienne in 1311–12 that attempted to get the Benedictines to wear black.

The very fact that this ecumenical council, surely one of the most obscure, concerned itself with the color of monastic clothing should indicate that something had changed, and not necessarily for the better. For example, the bishops gathered at Vienne decided that the monastic capuch or head covering should be a sort of scarf rather than the poncho most monks have always found more practical. Curiously, the Swiss and British monks have remained obedient to this odd regulation to this day. But the real significance of the decree of Vienne was that clothing had become a major concern for the whole church. Moreover, uniformity was now seen as imperative.

This attitude actually prevailed down to Vatican II, but after the Protestant Reformation it took on a different slant. If the Protestants got rid of monasticism as such, the Catholic Counter-Reformation would make sure not to change a single thing. Consequently it essentially clung to the medieval costume as a very prominent sign of its resistance to destructive change. It seems to me that in doing that the monks were engaging in what the Lutherans call "repristination," namely, a reversion to the past in the hope of putting a stop to change as such. Another well-known example of that would be the Hutterite refusal to accept any changes in clothing styles through the centuries.

The Meaning of Clothes for Monks

Since St. Benedict took a rather simple and pragmatic approach to clothing, and since I have been critical of subsequent monks for ignoring Benedict's lead in this matter, it may seem as if I too see clothing as simply a matter of keeping warm and modest. That is not my whole intent. Anybody who fails to see any symbolic significance in clothes is flying in the face of most of human history. Indeed, someone once said: our clothes are us. And this is not just a mythic or cultural question; it is very religious. Recall, if you will, the first chapters of the book of Genesis. What do Adam and Eve do after they have sinned? They put on fig leaves to hide their nakedness. And what does God do in response? He gives them "garments of skins" (Gen 3:21). Now surely that is not a mere throwaway line!

The monastic form of this wisdom saying is: Clothes make the monk: *habitus monachum facit.* Now of course the opposite is also invoked to make a good point: Clothes do *not* make the monk. It is quite possible to hide a corrupt life in a pious monastic habit. But generally speaking what we wear says something about us. And although Benedict was not particularly ideological in regard to clothes, he knew well enough that clothes make a statement. For example, in his ceremony of profession he takes the candidate's own clothes from him and issues him the "clothes of the monastery." If the person should be so foolish as to ever leave the community he must be stripped of the "clothes of the monastery" and given back his own clothes, which have been kept stored. Clearly we are dealing here with a definite uniform that shows that the monk belongs to *this* community and no other. It may not even be a peculiar style of clothing, but it should be recognized as belonging to the group and not the individual. This would seem to question any individualism in clothing.

That in itself is by no means insignificant, for some people feel a strong need to make an individual statement by their clothes. Surely one of the issues in the "clothing wars" many of the convents went through had to do with precisely this point. Many people felt a need to exert at least *some* personality in the matter of clothes. But we also have to recognize that the church wants us to wear something that shows that *we belong to the Order of consecrated persons.* We are simply not on our own, and we also are not lay people. We are monks and nuns, and we should look like monks and nuns.

But what do monks and nuns look like? That question is not so easy to answer. The easiest answer is no doubt to continue the tradition. But we should realize that the "tradition," at least in regard to clothes, refers only to the medieval period. If we insist on wearing a medieval garment, then we may be attempting to impersonate medieval people, which could be quite akin to functioning as models in a medieval theme park. If we do that we should not be too surprised if teachers bring their history classes to our monasteries to see what "monks look like." What they may mean is "this is what monks *used* to look like. And here we have some living relics."

How do we go about choosing a contemporary monastic habit? I would suggest that it must be at least three things: (1) It must be immediately recognizable by almost everybody; (2) it must be serviceable for everyday use; (3) it should be cheap and easily available.

The first item may be the most difficult. Let me suggest that the hood is probably the most evident sign of the monk for people in our society. Now someone will immediately counter with the valid point that nowadays lots of people wear hoods. That may very well be, but one could also say that they took the idea from monks in the first place. Besides, a real hood is a very useful thing to have in cold and windy climates like North Dakota.

The second point is perhaps the most important. A valid monastic habit should be appropriate for use just about anywhere. That means it is not primarily a liturgical garment but something one wears everywhere. Especially it should be able to be worn outside the monastery and throughout public society. Monastic men should put an end to their dysfunctional practice of jumping into civvies in order to go shopping. If we are too concerned not to create a "scene" in public we should ask ourselves whether we really are willing to function as public symbols of the Kingdom of God, for that is what the church wants us to do.

Finally, the question of cheap and easily available material is hardly beside the point. Benedict emphasized this matter and he had serious reasons. We should be a public witness to evangelical poverty. Is it not possible to find some kind of cloth that is both serviceable and yet "poor"? I would suggest that the best current candidate is denim, which is exactly what a few "reformed" monastic communities wear. A denim smock gathered by a belt seems to me to be a very respectable monastic garment. I doubt if many people in our society will fail to recognize this as some kind of religious symbol.

In closing, let me issue a necessary proviso. When I listed three aspects of a good modern religious habit I knew I was not creating a definitive series. For example, I said nothing about *beauty*. I do not want to imply that beauty is no consideration when it comes to monastic clothing. Certainly it was important for many religious through the ages, to judge from some of the splendid costumes they wore. But too often they became wildly impractical, fit only for the liturgy or maybe vocational advertising. Such a consideration greatly complicates this discussion.

Chapter Eleven

The Cell Phone and the Monk

The Cell Phone

One of the most remarkable technological inventions of recent times is the cell phone. Wherever you go, people have their hand up to their ear, and they are not scratching. You are driving the car through a busy intersection and you notice that many of the other drivers are talking on the phone. It does not increase your peace of mind. You are sitting in the airport early on Sunday morning and all at once someone near you begins shouting. He's not angry at you but at a business contact in Hong Kong. Then you notice that almost everybody else in the waiting room is also on the phone.

Once I was stuck in an airport during a flight delay. When the voice on the public address system announced that our plane would be taking off two hours late, many people, including me, groaned or cursed. But the girl sitting next to me knew exactly what to do. She whipped out her cell phone and began systematically calling a long list of friends. All the conversations, which I could not help but hear, went like this: "Hi. Oh, nothing. Just sitting in the airport waiting for a delayed plane. What are you up to?" and so on.

Now I have to confess right away that I do not own a cell phone. In fact, I have only used one a few times, and even then I had to have special instructions on how to manage it. Someone might say I am sour grapes because the monks in our community are not permitted to have these nearly obligatory modern devices. And there are indeed times when I wish

I had one. When I am driving on a lonely road and it is twenty below zero I get to feeling a bit vulnerable. It would also be good to have a cell phone in the airport to call the party waiting for me and tell them we have been delayed two hours. But by and large I feel no need for a cell phone. Moreover, I worry about certain aspects of our cell phone culture.

One concern is the non-stop chatting the cell phone promotes. Of course, some people have always liked to maintain a stream of chatter. It probably gives them some defense against the terrifying sense of loneliness they feel when they are alone. Besides, modern life is full of chatter, whether it be the television, the radio, or whatever. We seldom find ourselves in utter silence, and when we do we may experience it as quite disconcerting. Even some of our elder monks prefer to have a low level of noise around them at all times so they know everybody else in the house hasn't died.

The cell phone promotes chatter where none was previously possible. In the good old days, when you were walking down the street alone you kept quiet. You had no choice, for there was nobody within hearing range. Now, however, you can carry on a conversation in just about any circumstance—even in places where you really should be quiet. No doubt the economics of cell phone use promote this lavish use of the instrument. People seem to have unlimited minutes to use up, so there is little restraint on the amount of time they spend on the phone. I have a friend who is the monthly recipient of the gift of unlimited phone use anywhere in the world, so he spends every evening calling up all his friends and bending their ears. He tried that on me—once.

Obviously there are good reasons for talking on the phone. Business people seem to do little else but talk on the phone, so it is perfectly natural for them to continue doing it wherever they are, at least during the business day. Furthermore, the cell phone is useful for maintaining personal and family connections. To call home in the car and say "Start dinner, I'll be home in an hour" is a considerate thing to do. And far-flung families need to keep in touch if they are not to fall apart completely. But there is another element of cell phone culture that worries me even more. It has to do with presence and absence.

Whatever else we might say about the phone, when we are using it we are not completely present to where we are. We are talking to someone at a distance and our mind is necessarily with that person. Granted, we are still partially aware of our physical surroundings, but we cannot be fully present to them. Nowadays we use the rather nifty word "multitasking" and many people feel they can do several things at once. Students, for example, think they can listen to the radio or TV and still do their homework.

Teachers, however, can see the effects of partial concentration. Personally, as an editor I cannot even have music playing in the room when I am proof-reading. Total concentration for me demands cutting off all distractions.

By now most of us are aware of some of the truly tragic side effects of multitasking. We have probably heard about the passenger train wreck that recently killed dozens of people in California. The engineer ran a red light, and it did not help that he was texting on his cell phone at the time. He will now have eternity to contemplate his error. There are numerous reports of car wrecks in broad daylight in which the only possible cause can be cell phone use. Whether we admit it or not, we have only so much attention to spend, and the cell phone takes up a good deal of it.

It seems to me that the phenomenon of a bunch of people all talking on their cell phones instead of to one another is really a kind of foretaste of hell, or at least purgatory. Everybody is talking but nobody is actually present to the person in front of him. My confrère teaches at a local college. His class is three hours in the evening, so there are a couple of breaks where people used to go out into the hall to have a soft drink and chat. The trouble is, he says, that now they all go out there and talk on their cell phones! The other night he roundly excoriated them for this antisocial behavior when they returned, but they acted like he was talking Greek. We know that one of the issues with the Obama presidency was his refusal to completely put aside his Blackberry. Apparently this worried his staff very much.

We are rapidly approaching the point where nobody is actually fully present at any time. I went to a three-day meeting recently at which sixteen of us sat in a room for endless hours of intense dialogue on complicated issues. But not all of us: two of the members were constantly in and out of the room with their cell phones beeping. I was very near to making a nasty speech to this effect: "Why did you come here? Why not stay home? Don't you see how your constant shuttling in and out is disrupting our conversation?" It seems to me that this kind of antisocial behavior is having a seriously detrimental effect on human community in our time.

Utterly Flee Forgetfulness

What might St. Benedict have to say about the situation described above? Nothing directly, of course, because he never heard of a cell phone, blessed man. Nevertheless, I would propose to lift up a text from the Holy Rule that could have something to say to our current condition of widespread absentmindedness. This text comes from the first step of humility in RB 7, one of the premier chapters of the Rule:

> The first step of humility is to utterly flee forgetfulness by keeping the fear of God always before one's eyes. We must constantly recall the commandments of God, continually mulling over how hell burns the sinners who despise God, and eternal life is prepared for those who fear God. . . . Let each one take into account that he is constantly observed by God from heaven and our deeds everywhere lie open to the divine gaze and are reported by the angels at every hour. (RB 7.10-11, 13)

Before we get too distracted by the rather harsh tone of this text let me point out that the "fear of God" is used here in the classic biblical sense. It does not refer to abject terror in the face of a ferocious God, but rather to full awareness of the holiness of God. That is to say, God is God, not just another creature but the Creator of the universe who is quite above and beyond the world. But this same God is not therefore absent. Far from it! He is present everywhere, right here and now. What is more, he is fully aware of me. Furthermore, God is not aloof or neutral. He has expectations of his creation, which means you and me. His commandments are meant to be taken seriously, and if we refuse or neglect to do so we will have to take the consequences.

One runs the risk of turning off the modern reader with such an unfashionable quotation from St. Benedict. Isn't he supposed to be the gentle, moderate father of monks? What is wrong with him here? Did he get up on the wrong side of the bed? Besides, contemporary Catholicism has largely abandoned this kind of in-your-face talk about sin and damnation. Those of us over sixty heard plenty of it in our youth, but since Vatican II, Catholic preachers and teachers have considerably toned down these themes.

Yet I would not want to suggest that this passage is uncharacteristic of St. Benedict. In fact, this same cluster of ideas about God's omnipresence as judge turns up no fewer than four times in the Rule (4.44-63; 7.10-13; 7.26-30; 19.1-3). In fact, it is so pervasive that I did not hesitate to pinpoint it as the heart of Benedict's spirituality in a recent article. But I quickly added that Benedict also makes sure we realize that this uncompromising God is especially present in the weakest and most marginal persons in society. So when we discount the poor and lowly we are indeed playing with heavenly fire!

This daunting theme of God's threatening presence is no invention of St. Benedict. In fact, it is mostly material he copied from the Rule of the Master. And that dour, forbidding author himself got it from a much older source, namely, the Rule of St. Basil. Therefore Jean Gribomont was partly right when he claimed that St. Basil is the primary spiritual source for Benedict's Rule. Anybody who has read Basil's Rule and his other works knows that he is no lightweight. Indeed, the hallmark of Basil is utter moral seriousness. After all, he was the one who insisted that to break one commandment was to break them all. So he combed the New Testament for all Jesus' commandments, and he found about 1,500 of them! (See *Moral Rules.*)

For our discussion here I want to focus on the words "forgetfulness" and "recall." In Latin these are wonderfully resonant terms: *oblivio* and *memoria.* The first step of humility according to Benedict is for us to "keep in mind" and "utterly flee forgetfulness." We have already spoken about what we are to be acutely aware of, namely, God and all that he demands of us. But first of all we must wake up spiritually and become fully aware of where we are and what we are faced with. This is the ultimate wake-up call.

I would like to cast my net a bit further out and note that awareness of the present is a hallmark of Zen Buddhism. I used to teach history of religions, and once I remember showing a fine little Buddhist film called simply "Awareness." The message of that film was the need for the spiritual person to become fully aware of the present moment. After all, it is the only moment we have, since the past is gone and the future is not yet here. But when we actually try to focus on the present we find it much slipperier than we might have imagined.

One way Zen novice masters try to teach awareness is by helping their students to concentrate on ordinary mundane activities. Their intensive meditation has the same purpose, but when it comes to everyday activity the Buddhist novice is urged to pay very strict attention to the way she does things. For example, when she is pouring tea she does not do it just any old way. No, there is a proper way to pour tea, and that must be mastered. First of all one must be fully present to this utterly mundane activity; otherwise the tea gets spilled. And there is also a right way and a wrong way to wash a leaf of lettuce. You start by respecting that leaf of lettuce, which is hard for us to do in a consumerist society where the dumpsters are full of perfectly good leaves of lettuce.

When I was a novice a long, long time ago (1956), it seemed to me that my novice-master was largely concerned about the wrong things. For example, one day I knocked on his door and entered his office. "Now go back out and do it properly," he said. I had no idea what he was talking about, so he then showed me how to knock on a door, how to turn the knob and then close it behind myself. He made me practice this routine several times, and he made me do it over again on several other occasions. At the time I felt all this was a lot of pickiness merely designed to teach me humility. But after fifty years I now am ready to reconsider it.

In those simple days the novitiate was even simpler. We were spared a lot of distractions by being closed off from the outside world. We were allowed to read no newspapers, make no telephone calls, and receive no visitors. As for cell phones and Blackberries and e-mail, forget it. They did not exist, and if they had we would not have been allowed to use them. Certainly there was very little multitasking in that novitiate. When you had to pour the abbot's soup you had nothing else to worry about. Even so, I managed to spill a tureen of gravy down his scapular one day. Maybe my mind was not as uncluttered as it should have been.

But it would not be good to depart too far from our original text here and we should not forget that according to Benedict the object of our awareness should be the presence of God. As the Christian Brothers used to pray before every class: "Let us remember that we are in the presence of God!" Yet it may also seem as if there is some contradiction here. How can we remain focused on the present moment and the present circumstances if we are fully mindful of God, who is not present in any objective, physical way? As can be seen in many of the lives of the saints, people sometimes become so wrapped in contemplation of God that they become unable to function properly in the present. As my friend Kathleen Norris once said to me: "No poet should drive a car!"

In order to grapple a bit with this seeming conundrum let me refer to another short passage from the Rule, this time on the monk's behavior at the Divine Office:

> We believe that God is present everywhere and that the "eyes of the Lord gaze everywhere on the good and bad." We should, though, be totally convinced that this is so when we are present at the Divine Office. . . . So let us be careful how we behave in the sight of God and his angels. And let us stand to sing in such a way that our mind is in harmony with our voice. (RB 19.1-2, 6-7)

In order to provide a bit of background to this passage let me point out that the ancient monks liked to fill their day with the psalms. Typically they memorized dozens of psalms so they could recite them all day long: at work, while walking, while eating, and so on. Most of their work was made up of simple, repetitive tasks and was quite unlike the complicated work many modern people do. If it were not simple I think they would have risked schizophrenia.

At this point someone might interject that this looks precisely like the multitasking I have been criticizing in this essay. In fact, it was quite the opposite. They knew their work could be so boring and stultifying that their minds were prone to fill up with all kinds of troublesome nonsense. This is what they called "*logismoi*," thoughts. The way they worked against the bad thoughts was to replace them with good thoughts in the form of biblical texts. Thus they filled their memory tapes with the psalms. This could have the effect of making them mindful, and not forgetful, of the presence of God.

The text of RB 19 is about something specific, namely, the Divine Office. Here the problem is a bit different. We are asked to keep our minds in harmony with our voices. In other words, we are to remain aware of what we are singing or reciting. Fair enough: woolgathering or gazing around surely do not come up to the standard of participation expected in the Christian liturgy. Moreover, the words we are singing in the Divine Office are by and large the words of the Bible, so it is all the more fitting that we pay attention to what we are saying. Yet this is not such a simple matter as it might seem.

The problem, as I see it, is at least twofold. On the one hand it takes a good deal of concentration and also stamina to participate in the monastic choir prayer in a proper manner. The music itself, especially difficult music like Gregorian Chant and its derivatives, demands concentration. And sometimes the words are fairly intricate, so that we need to be very careful to negotiate the sentences properly. But even when we do we are faced with the demands of choir participation, and they are not negligible. We must keep together with the other monks, we must subdue our egos to serve the group effort, we must work harder when the choir is weak, and so forth.

But let's say we can manage all of this without too much effort. Many monks know the psalms and melodies by heart, so they do not need to struggle with them. It all flows easily enough. Still, there is the considerable problem of pacing. Since the Office must flow right along, it is not possible for the individual to linger on any word or phrase. Consequently there really is not much possibility of any kind of comprehension in depth during the choral prayer. Prolonged meditation on the text is out of the question. Some communities pause between the psalms, and that certainly helps. And most communities in the USA now recite the psalms rather slowly, which also helps. But "mind in harmony with voice" still cannot mean full comprehension when applied to the Divine Office.

When in 1970 or thereabouts our monasteries were permitted to switch from the Latin to the vernacular, many of us thought this would help a great deal in the Office. We were not all that skilled at parsing the Latin and we thought that the language was itself the problem. But after almost forty years of vernacular Office I have to say I have not found English to be the panacea I had hoped for. The Office still flies by, and I really cannot say that I am very often able to penetrate it to any depth.

But I am also beginning to doubt whether that is what we really should be aiming for in the Office. Granted, we do not want to let our minds wander all over the place. That can happen, of course, but I don't find my mind off on a trip during the Office. I am concentrating, but I am not exegeting the psalm in front of me. I am not even thinking pious thoughts. I am just trying to stay present to the Liturgy and fully engaged in the choral effort. This is not a matter of multitasking. We haven't brought cell phones into the monastic choir—yet. We surely believe that God is especially present and active in this Liturgy that is being done expressly for the honor and glory of God. We are mindful; we are not forgetful.

Chapter Twelve   *Table Reading*

Anyone who has had a meal with the monks in a monastic refectory (dining room) has probably had a memorable experience. Instead of the usual table talk one has at an ordinary meal, in the monastery meals are usually taken in silence while listening to a book being publicly read. Such a thing might also take place somewhere else, but table reading is an experience nearly unique to the monastery.

It is also an ancient monastic practice. Benedict has a whole chapter on the subject (RB 38), but it was already a regular monastic custom long before his time. Indeed, one of Benedict's favorite monastic sources, Basil of Caesarea (ca. 370), already had his monks read at table. The same can be said for Augustine of Hippo about twenty-five years later. Since these are two of the "pillars of cenobitism," that is, founders of communal monastic life, Benedict thinks table reading is important for his monastic enterprise.

Why do the monks read at table? There are all kinds of good reasons, which we discuss in the following considerations. But it must also be admitted that table reading has its price. Someone like the author who has spent much of his monastic life listening to table reading knows that it can degenerate into a kind of antithesis of what it should be. But I would prefer to wait with my criticisms of the practice until I have examined St. Benedict's own arrangements for table reading.

RB 38: On the Weekly Reader

From the very title we can tell that Benedict takes table reading seriously. He appoints this person "to serve for a week," and not just at random. This suggests that he wants the reader to approach his work in a systematic and careful way. He makes this same point in a formal way by repeating it in the first and last verses of this well-constructed chapter. This is called an *inclusion*, and it occurs throughout ancient literature, including the Bible. Benedict also makes this point in a more explicit manner: "The meals of the brothers ought not to lack reading, nor should just anyone who happens to pick up the book read there" (RB 38.1). Note that he manages to include in the same sentence a principle and an anecdotal example.

Another way Benedict underlines the importance of table reading lies in his instruction that the weekly reader receive a blessing in church after the Sunday liturgy. The kitchen staff also is blessed at this time, so it seems clear that Benedict wants to make a connection between worship and meals. Of course, we know that "church" for Catholics involves a table for Mass and communion. We usually call that an altar, but we should not forget that it also centers on a ritual meal, namely, the Holy Eucharist. By having the blessing of the reader and waiter immediately after communion Benedict wants to show that the ordinary meal itself should have a sacramental quality about it.

If the table reader has such an important job, what are his qualifications? Reading is not like some other monastic jobs that can be done by almost anyone. "The brothers are not to read or sing in order, but only those who edify the listeners" (RB 38.12). At a basic level we might say that Benedict wants readers who can actually read. I once got taken down a peg or two by a friend of mine who was a professional drama coach. After a Mass I had celebrated he made some comment about "miserable readers." I chimed in with him about the *other* readers, but he brought me up short with: "and that includes you." I think of myself as a good public reader, so I pressed him to point out my shortcomings. After he did, I ceased to think of myself as a good public reader.

Of course, this man was a professional speech coach, and Benedict cannot expect professional reading from his monks. What *does* he expect? One simple word makes the point: edification. This is not a very common English word, and even if we know its general meaning we may not be aware of its rich connotations. To edify is often taken to mean that we cause another person to have some kind of religious experience, or at least we make them feel good. But edification in Latin means "building up." That can refer to an individual, but it can also refer to a community. I think Benedict wants table reading that will build up the whole community and not tear it apart. That could have many implications, of course, but in general we don't want a table reader who will irritate us or upset us while we are eating. A meal should never be a time of tension.

It may also help to examine the concrete circumstances of reading at the time of Benedict. In the sixth century there were no printed books. Readers were faced with manuscripts, hand-written texts with all their idiosyncrasies. Usually they were written by expert scribes, but they rarely had the reader-friendly features we now expect in printed texts. For example, the punctuation was erratic and often not much help. What is more, there was often no spacing between the words! All this made it imperative that the reader do advance preparation for his work. To presume to read without preparation was a formula for embarrassment.

For his part, Benedict was aware that public reading is not an easy job. He was sympathetic to the special problems of the reader, no doubt because of personal experience. Thus we find this rather humane provision: "The brother who is the weekly reader should receive some watered wine before he reads. This is because of the Holy Communion and because he may find it difficult to endure the fast. He should eat with the weekly cooks and servers after the meal" (RB 38.10-11). This is a good example of St. Benedict's essential humanity. Of course, some of this is connected to the fact that Benedict's monks had their meal right after communion. That meant a lengthy fast, enough to weaken the average person. The readers deserve a drink of some kind in preparation for this work.

Depending on the circumstances, table reading can still be hard work. In the refectory of my monastery the reader was stationed in the middle of a long, narrow room. For him to reach both ends with his voice could be a challenge, especially before we installed a public address system. To make it even worse, the reader faced out a large door into a hallway! It sometimes seemed to me that they were determined to make it as hard as possible for the poor reader. Yet most of us who did the reading were also preparing for a lifetime of preaching and teaching. A strong, clear voice is imperative for such a person.

Benedict is also aware that the diners have their own responsibility to help the table reader. Here is what he says: "Profound silence should reign there, so that the only voice heard will be that of the reader and not of anyone else whispering or talking" (RB 38.5). Obviously, if there is enough chattering going on the reader is faced with a real obstacle. As it is, even in the quietest of monastic refectories there is still the ground noise of dining: clattering dishes and silverware and so forth. Nothing can eliminate this clatter, but at least Benedict wants to keep refectory noise down to a minimum.

Before we leave this section on ancient table reading we might add a few items that help to place Benedict's arrangements in some kind of interpretative context. It is interesting to note that there is an important lacuna in the history of monastic table reading, namely, Egypt. The Pachomian communities had meals in common, but it seems they were always taken in silence. Furthermore, there are certain aspects of those meals that indicate that Pachomius had a sort of penitential attitude toward the very act of eating. For example, he insists that the monks eat with their cowls up so they will not be able to observe anyone else eating (Pr. 31). If this is indeed a sign of Pachomius's basic embarrassment with eating, and some scholars deny that it is, at least we can say that Benedict shows no signs of discomfort with things of the body, and certainly not in regard to meals.

One monastic founder who appreciated table reading was Augustine of Hippo. In his Garden Monastery, close by the cathedral, they read at table. What is more, in his Rule for Monks, Augustine gives his reasons for insisting on table reading: it prevents quarrels and it nourishes the soul (Rule 3.2). The last point is the more important of the two, and we might wish that Benedict had said something to that effect in his chapters on monastic meals (RB 35–41). To put it even more nicely, Basil of Caesarea says that the soul should be fed as well as the body (Short Rules 180).

When Augustine became the bishop of Hippo he made different arrangements for meals. He required the local clergy to live with him, and he replaced table reading with conversation—but not just any kind of conversation. Augustine hated gossip and took steps to make sure it would not prevail at his table. In his biography of Augustine his protégé Possidius of Calama records that the bishop was so allergic to gossip that he had carved on his table a saying to the effect that if they insisted on gossiping he would eat elsewhere! This reminds us of Martin Luther's behavior when arguing with Zwingli about the Eucharist. Well aware that Zwingli was a spellbinder, Luther wrote on the table: "This *is* my body!" Of course, Luther was a fervent Augustinian.

One more monastic source we might examine is the Rule of the Master. When we dip into that long and sometimes bizarre Rule we find plenty on the meals of the community. Basically, the Master has the same arrangements as Benedict in that he always has table reading at meals. But one big difference lies in the Master's practice of encouraging open discussion of the reading at table. He wants the disciples to ask questions about it, and he urges the abbot to expatiate at length in a kind of Platonic symposium event (RM 24.26-37). We get the overall impression that the Master's table was a fairly wild, chaotic scene.

If that is what it was, Benedict wanted no part of it. He forbids the brothers from asking questions, and he tells the abbot to keep his remarks to a minimum. He does not want to "give the devil an opening" (RB 38.8). Apparently Benedict had enough experience with table talk to know it could get out of hand. But beyond that, he does not think of his abbot in the way the Master does. The Master's abbot spends most of his time lecturing, but Benedict's abbot is more reticent.

Moreover, the two Rules have different kinds of reading at table. The Master limits his community to listening to the *Rule of the Master*! He wants that document read over and over. It does not seem to occur to him that this might get tiresome. Benedict, however, probably wants the Bible read at table. He never specifies the content of the reading, but we can infer that the Bible was at least part of the daily table reading. Of course, there is a good deal more variety in the Bible than in just the *Rule of the Master*. In fact, there are vast tracts of the Bible that most people never ever encounter, even in church.

In my own experience I remember as a novice being quite shaken when I heard certain parts of the prophet Ezekiel read in the dining room. First of all, I could not believe that such things were present in the Bible (naked babies abandoned by the side of the road, etc.), so it led me to check it out for myself. Sure enough, there they were. But then I remember my censorious superego clucking that really such things should not be read at table! Well, maybe they shouldn't be in the Bible either, but they are. The regular practice of table reading can teach us some things we never knew before.

Taking a Broader Look at Meals

The Bible itself teaches us that meals are very important. As in any healthy traditional culture, the Jews knew the great significance of the group meal. For all these people it was a primary means of expressing solidarity and community. In that society who you ate with and why you ate with them meant a great deal. Consequently, when the Hebrews were liberated from Egyptian slavery by God they were commanded to commemorate the event by celebrating a special meal together. As we learn in Exodus 12, this meal was to be repeated every year on the anniversary of the liberation, and it was to include the recital of what happened originally. In other words, it was a meal with a script.

Like all traditional societies, the Jews did not practice "open commensality"; they refused to sit down at table with non-Jews. From a Western point of view this could be seen as a sign of a narrow, warped view of human relations, but for them the meal was a sacred symbol that had to carry a heavy moral freight. Still at the time of Jesus, Jews were not in the habit of eating with "unclean" (ritually impure) people. One of the most serious accusations against Jesus was "he eats with sinners and tax-collectors" (Mark 2:16). A famous biblical scholar used to say that Jesus was ultimately executed "because he ate with the wrong people."

Since meals were so important, not to say enjoyable, it should be no surprise that they imagined the messianic era or salvation would be like a great feast. Here is what we read in Isaiah 25:

> On this mountain the LORD of hosts will make for all peoples a feast of fat things, a feast of wine on the lees, of fat things full of marrow, of wine on the lees well refined. And he will destroy on this mountain the covering that is cast over all peoples, the veil that is spread over all nations. He will swallow up death for ever, and the Lord GOD will wipe away tears from all faces, and the reproach of his people he will take away from all the earth; for the LORD has spoken. (Isa 25:6-9)

This particular description of the great final banquet contains some details we might not appreciate, like wine-lees and fat things full of marrow. Yet everybody with a normal human background has experienced a fancy meal at which the table was loaded down with delicacies, the kind Norman Rockwell used to illustrate on the covers of the *Saturday Evening Post*.

But in order to really appreciate such a passage it is probably necessary to know something about ordinary peasant life in ancient times. Those were not people who saw very many fancy meals. Most of them got enough to eat, but it was pretty basic fare—black bread, grains and beans, etc. Nevertheless, banquets were not unknown in those societies. Indeed, it was a pretty wretched village that could not set out a communal feast at least a couple of times a year. This was a time when people made up for their usual frugal meals. For example, there was always plenty of meat, which was virtually absent from their everyday diet.

A professor once told us that when he was a graduate student at the American Academy in Rome in the 1930s he used to bicycle out to some of the hill towns near the city to observe village life. He said that one day he happened to be present at a village banquet, probably on the feast day of the local patron saint. At any rate there was a family sitting near him and one of the little boys was obviously famished and was really tearing into the pasta. But his father admonished the poor kid, telling him not to waste space on pasta but to wait for the meat course. That's what really counts! It was a valuable lesson for a youngster who would probably not see too much meat the rest of his life.

Since traditional life in the Mediterranean had not changed much from the time of Moses to the time of Jesus we should expect that the Lord would also take meals seriously. In fact, the gospels often picture him at table with his friends, with tax-collectors, with Pharisees, and so on. Moreover, some of his most memorable sayings and miracles take place while he is at table. We get the impression that for the circles in which

Jesus moved meals and parties were a normal part of life. That was where you encountered people, where you told them who you were and where you learned who they were. These were not our rushed, frenetic meals, but leisurely, open-ended meals like those that can still be observed in neighborhood *trattorie* in Italy to this day.

There was one special meal in Jesus' life, a meal at which he presided as the host. This took place sometime around the Passover and probably was connected to the Seder meal. At any rate we know that Jesus turned this festive banquet into something more, something absolutely transcendental. He took bread and said "This is my body." He also took up the cup filled with wine and declared "This is my blood." Surely the disciples present on that occasion could not have taken in the depth of that symbolic meal. They did not yet have the Holy Spirit. Actually, we who *do* have the Holy Spirit, and who have had two thousand years to think about it, still are merely scratching the surface of what he meant! But this much is certain: he used a meal to symbolize his basic relationship to the human race.

Pulling back a bit from the Bible, let us think a bit about meals as such. I don't think it would be too much to claim that meals are a primary human symbol. As such, they are not something that should be tampered with or degraded. We need to be vigilant against various kinds of inroads on our meals. For example, some years ago I was staying with my cousins in California, people with whom I shared a lot of basic attitudes toward life. Imagine my dismay when I found that our meals were polluted with the blaring of a large television set near the table. It made normal conversation impossible, and it nearly drove me berserk. Apparently I had traveled two thousand miles to visit a TV set! The very idea of making the TV the focus while we ate seemed to me outrageous. What about the food? What about each other?

Yet the whole idea of conversation at meals is not to be taken for granted. It simply does not exist in some families. When my niece's husband joined our extended family he was astounded to find the whole group conversing during the meal and then lingering afterward to do so. He said it almost scared him, and it took him a while to get used to. Well, what did they do in his family? They just filled up their plates from the stove and stood around gobbling until they were finished. This just goes to prove that table conversation is not a human given. We learn it at the family table, and if we don't we have to learn it as adults.

Or do we? We hear that family meals are becoming increasingly precarious. Families are so terribly busy that they cannot find a time when they can all sit down together. The main culprit is children's sports. Every child has to be at this practice or that tournament, and that means the parents have to ferry them around. It appears we have gotten ourselves so ridiculously overscheduled that we have no actual time for family life. If we are too busy for common meals we are simply too busy. We are killing ourselves, and we are letting our kids kill themselves. If we don't teach children how to sit down and enjoy a leisurely meal we are robbing them of basic human training.

To return to our specific subject of monastic table reading, we should ask how it relates to the question of healthy human meals. I don't see how we can avoid asking why the early monks, and most subsequent monks, deliberately chose to set aside the normal way of eating for something else. For them to eschew table conversation was to break with a custom followed all over the world. Of course, monks have always been countercultural in that they do not simply live like the rest of humanity. They deliberately forego basic human practices like marriage and ownership of property in the name of a higher good. Looked at this way, monastic table reading is a break with the normal, healthy way of eating.

Before we assent too glibly to altering such an important human practice, however, we ought to ask if table conversation really is something we can do without. Since the common meal is perhaps the quintessential means of building up human community we have to be careful about doing anything to undermine this practice. Remember that our whole society is currently abandoning healthy eating practices, with the result that those who come to the monastery nowadays do not necessarily know how to have a decent meal. We may have to teach them this fine art, and it could be that table reading will be part of the problem, not the solution.

You might ask what I have against table reading. Just this: too often it turns meals into races in which the slow, deliberate eater is penalized or even urged to hurry up. At least in traditional table reading practice, at a certain point the abbot rings his bell, the reader cuts off his palaver, the monks rise and pray, and all file out of the refectory. In the abstract that doesn't sound too ominous, but in lived reality it can be a bit brutal. If, for example, the superior is a fast eater he might sit there with his hand on the bell glaring at those who are still working on their meal. In large monasteries family-style dining means that the most junior monks receive their food last; therefore they are always under the gun to get finished. It does not make for peaceful digestion. Nowadays most monasteries solve this problem by cutting off the reading about two-thirds through the meal. That way those who simply must bolt their food and run can do so if they choose. Others, who prefer to eat in a more relaxed manner, can also do so.

Actually, most monasteries today do not have reading at every meal. If they do they should realize that such a practice is probably having at least one harmful effect on their members, namely, they tend to forget how to carry on a normal meal conversation. Probably someone will wonder why that is so important. It is important because it is one of the recognized skills of a civilized person. A person who does not know how to eat and talk is going to be out of place at a civilized dinner should he ever be invited to one. In years past it was not unusual to see a monk bolting his food while others casually conversed and then waiting impatiently for them to finish. He had forgotten how to eat.

Moreover, I think it is quite important for monasteries to have at least occasional festal meals. I am talking about three- or four-course dinners, with wine and other special elements. Such a meal takes time to work through, but I don't think anybody should be allowed to leave before everybody else is finished. Such a meal is not a mere question of refueling; it is an important part of community building. People who find such meals tedious have a right to their opinion, but they are showing signs of lacking basic human sensibilities. And certainly there must be *no* table reading at such a meal.

Chapter Thirteen   *Competition*

In 1 Corinthians 9:24 St. Paul says that all run but only one wins the prize. In saying this he sounds like a typical modern American extolling the values of competition. Actually he is not engaging in thoroughgoing exaltation of competition. He is just urging the Corinthians to strive hard to win a heavenly reward by a good Christian life. Paul's casual excursion into competitive language is set in the familiar language of sports: "Do you not know that in a race all the runners compete, but only one receives the prize? Run so as to win" (RSV). So it is quite clear that Paul and his audience were familiar with "big time athletics." They knew about stadiums and races and prizes. No doubt their stadiums were comparatively small, their races fairly slow, and their prizes moderate, but it was still a competitive atmosphere.

Competition in Contemporary Culture

This same interest in competitive sports has continued to our own day. Indeed, it has become almost an epidemic among us, a religion, if you will. Some people in our society plunge into intense athletic training at a young age, so much so that they seem to forfeit their childhood. These are the expert participants in our big-time sports, but most of us are spectators. Yet that does not mean that we are uninvolved. In fact, some cities and regions live and die with the fortunes of their athletic teams.

This kind of passionate interest in competitive sports has some side effects that are good and some that are not so good. It is hard to argue against the effort and discipline young people put into sports. It has to make them stronger people. And sports can teach us many useful human

106

values: cooperation, fairness, even compassion. However, we should not exaggerate the last, because competitive sports always imply losers, and losers are not appreciated in our society.

Because they are glamorous and stimulating, high-level sports also tend to attract big money. When you see people walking around wearing New York Yankees caps and jackets you should know that those items cost twice as much as ordinary clothing. And that kind of adulation goes on worldwide, so a tidal wave of money now flows into big-time sports. Where there is money, corruption is not far behind. We know that addictive gambling is associated with sports, and so is the use of chemicals that can eventually ruin the athlete's body.

If anyone doubts that competition is one of the chief values in our society I would invite you to accompany me into church on a given Sunday. Periodically I find myself questioning the value of competition in a sermon. And when I do that I invariably find visitors in the sacristy after Mass. These people are not there to discuss the Trinity or the Incarnation. They do not even care how I interpret the Scriptures. What they don't like is for anybody to gore their sacred cow of competition. That's going too far.

Although people object to someone questioning the sacredness of competitive sports, one suspects that they are also nervous about the economic implications of this criticism, for competition is an indispensable component of our capitalist economy. This is not something one has to argue or defend in our culture. Everyone knows that the world of business and finance absolutely demands competition. This is the so-called Marketplace that is held in such high regard by so many people in our Western society. God help anyone who criticizes the Marketplace.

These people may exaggerate, but they have a point. Anyone who refuses to compete is not going to do well in our economy. This became glaringly clear with the fall of communism in Eastern Europe. Although most of us naïvely assumed the citizens of Russia and Poland and Hungary would just love to escape the iron hand of the totalitarian government and plunge into the free economic world of capitalism, that did not prove to be the case. In fact, after seventy years of a planned economy few of them have any taste for competition. Rather, they find it very stressful and even deadly. So capitalism is not exactly booming in Eastern Europe.

Of course, the obverse of this is the dismal condition of the economies in the former communist zone. Since there were guaranteed jobs, and economic decisions were made by higher-ups, little initiative was required. There was a saying: "You pretend to work, and we'll pretend to pay you." It could be that sports were emphasized so fervently in those countries just to give people something to live for, to bring some element of excitement to their drab lives.

Why is competition exhilarating, at least for many people? No doubt there are all kinds of reasons, some of which are more basic than others. Charles Darwin, for example, discovered that the progress of the natural world is essentially a competition between species. He saw that natural history is basically a matter of the survival of the fittest, with the weaklings regularly eliminated. From a biological standpoint this makes good sense, but when it gets translated into social policy by people like Nietzsche and Hitler it doesn't sound so fine. And Jesus in his Gospel rejects it entirely.

Another theory of competition is sometimes called *mimesis*. This is a Greek term used by some scholars to refer to the psychological mechanism we often call envy. With *mimesis*, which literally means imitation, people learn what to want by watching other people. More specifically, they only appreciate what other people have and they don't have. Thus begins the struggle for goods and honors. The root of this thinking is the assumption that life is a zero-sum game, a situation of scarcity in which there is not enough to go around. The only way to function successfully in such a world is to push hard for what you want. If other people have to lose it so you can have it, too bad for them.

All this sounds somewhat drastic and pessimistic, like a dog-eat-dog world. But I do not hesitate to point to this aspect of capitalism for the simple reason that it seems to have gotten us into a terrible fix at present. For some time now, at least in this country, smart and rich people have been preaching a philosophy of economic selfishness. The government was told to stay out of the way so the titans of big business could run the world in an efficient way. Unfortunately, that system has now been revealed for what it always was: a cover-up for unbridled greed. But it also failed, and we have a serious recession that currently leaves many people out of work.

Then we had CEOs converging on Congress bearing tin cups for handouts. The government was expected to rescue the failed rich (which it by and large did). There was no more talk of competition and the Marketplace, but rather a plea for mercy. This is not to claim that competition in itself brought us to this sorry place. But *capitalisme sauvage*, dog-eat-dog economic competition, had a big part in this fiasco. Perhaps now we are ready to consider that there might be some other human values worth appreciating. I think we can turn to St. Benedict for some of those insights.

Competition in the Rule of Benedict

When I was a student in the boarding school at Assumption Abbey in the 1950s we had a lot of close contact with the monks. Not only were they our classroom teachers and our prefects in the dormitory; sometimes they also allowed us to work with them and play with them. On weekends we would pick potatoes or pour concrete with a monastic crew; we would also engage in pick-up basketball games with them. In this way we got to know the monks on a rather intimate, experiential level that attracted some of us finally to join the monastic community.

One of the traits of the monks that I liked best was their spirit of brotherliness. Of course we knew they were all officially members of the same monastic community, but they actually lived this out in ways that went quite beyond the realm of rarified spirituality. One aspect of their brotherliness was their utter lack of rivalry or competitiveness with one another. As far as I can remember we never heard a monk tear down another monk behind his back. There was no obvious jockeying for positions of power in the school. In short, they were a peaceful social body.

Now that I am a monk myself, and a student of the Rule of St. Benedict, I think it is clear enough in the Rule itself that this lack of competitiveness is what Benedict wants of his disciples. To illustrate that I propose to lift up two chapters, one somewhat theoretical and idealistic, the other more practical.

First let us look at RB 72, "On the Good Zeal of Monks." This chapter starts out with the programmatic statement that there are two kinds of zeal: a bad zeal of bitterness that leads to hell and a good zeal that leads to God and to heaven. This may seem like a platitude, but in connection with our topic here, namely, competitiveness, we should note that zeal is at the heart of the question. People who like to compete with other people, or who *must* do so, are full of the basic energy we call zeal. Without this fire in the belly there is no competition.

Benedict knows, too, that this same zeal is at the heart of religion. Without a passionate attachment to God and to good, religion is just a boring round of formalities. Yet the author of the Rule also knows that the very energy that makes for good religion can also wreak havoc in the human community. That is why he hastens to define good zeal: "Thus monks should practice this (good) zeal with the warmest love." As I have said elsewhere and often, my translation of *ferventissimo* as "warmest" is not an exaggeration. This is exactly what the text says.

But what does he mean by such language? Is it simply purple prose, not meant to be taken literally? I would respond that it is exactly the opposite. In some of the ensuing verses in this little chapter Benedict shows that he has very concrete ideas about the good zeal monks should have toward one another. Anybody who claims that this chapter is basically a sort of pious flight of rhetoric must then tell us how to take similar passages in the New Testament, for RB 72 is basically a paraphrase of Saint Paul's teachings on mutual love.

This becomes clear in the very next verse: "Let them strive to be the first to honor one another" (72.4). First we should notice that we have here the language of competition. Rendered literally it means "they should go before one another." The verb *praeveniant* means to run faster, to outstrip. In the archaic English translation they were still reading in the monastic dining room when I was a novice it said: "They should prevent one another in honor." That made no sense at all to me; in fact, it sounded like the antithesis of Christian charity.

When Paul and Benedict say that we should outdo each other in paying honor they may well be consciously engaging in a sly "deconstruction" of the idea of competition. In other words, they are urging us to be the first in line—in order to defer to the other. This oxymoronic language of a competition in deference has the effect of turning competition on its head. Instead of striving frantically to achieve the first place for ourselves, here we go the extra mile on behalf of others.

Although it is hard to imagine a text like this one in a humorous vein, let me refer to another monastic Rule that makes this point even more baldly. In his Rule for monks St. Basil runs a kind of question-and-answer service in which he responds to typical monastic questions—sort of a cenobitic Ann Landers column. Some monks report that they are having a problem in their community with Jesus' injunction to take the last place at the banquet (see Luke 14:10). This is causing problems because the monks are fighting over the last place in the assembly. Without blinking at this ridiculous situation Basil solemnly tells them that such competition is quite unseemly. Each one must take his assigned place, even if it is the highest place! Such is true cenobitic humility.

To make sure we understand that he really means this teaching on Christian striving in love Benedict rephrases the point in verse six: "They must compete with one another in obedience." The salient word here is actually the Latin adverb *certatim*, which means "in a competitive manner." The point is quite the same. To be the most obedient monk means to put the good of other people first. Indeed, Benedict follows this with a verse that says it again in even starker terms: "No one should pursue what he judges advantageous to himself, but rather what benefits others." This is pure altruism of the kind that some modern critics do not believe exists. They think we *always* act out of self-interest whether we know it or not. Benedict, however, is not afflicted with that kind of cynicism. He thinks we really can put others first.

To get back to the question of obedience, it is a crucial issue in all the monastic Rules. With Saint Benedict obedience usually means deferring to the superior or at least to a monastic senior, that is, a monk with a higher rank. In the preceding chapter, that is, RB 71, Benedict attempts to discuss "mutual obedience." I say "attempts" because I do not think he is very successful. He starts out all right: "The blessing of obedience is not only something that everyone ought to show to the abbot, but the brothers should also obey one another." This sounds fine, but he soon gets distracted by the problem of conflicting commands and ends by thundering against a junior monk ever daring to question his senior about anything.

Benedict's ambivalence in RB 71 is not surprising. In fact, mutual obedience is not an easy thing to understand, much less put into practice. It refers to a basic orientation toward life and toward other people. If I am mutually obedient I am essentially open to what other people have to teach me. They may disappoint me, but I think I have something to learn from everybody, from the abbot to the candidate. What is more, I don't see life as a jungle where you have to "get them before they get you." It is true that this kind of trust in other people can appear naïve, and it can also be betrayed. But to approach life and other people as a zero-sum game in which I must fight for my rights—that seems incompatible with the Gospel of Jesus and the Rule of Benedict.

We might ask the further question of how Benedict actually implemented such an ideal of mutual obedience. One window on that matter is seen in the choice of the abbot. Benedict thinks this is such an important matter that he devotes an entire chapter (64) to it. The first half of that chapter discusses abbatial elections and the second half outlines what sort of person he wants for the abbot of his community.

When we study the abbatial selection process in RB 64 we are struck by at least two things. First, Benedict says that the ordinary way to choose an abbot is for the whole community to agree on the selection. But he also suggests it may be better for a smaller group of sounder judgment to make the choice. We wonder who decides who is of sounder judgment? Over the long haul of monastic history abbots have been chosen by all sorts of methods, from election to outright appointment by a higher official. Nowadays we usually elect our own abbot, but in special cases he is still appointed. Benedict knows that the choice of a superior can go disastrously wrong, so he makes provision for the intervention of outside parties such as the local bishop.

But another element in this process is more to the point here: Benedict makes no mention of competition in regard to the abbatial election. How can this be? In a sense it is perfectly natural, since the Rule sets up humility as one of the principal virtues of the monk. Such humility would seem to rule out any ambition on the part of the monk for authority or power. So if the monks were all perfectly humble, none of them would desire to be abbot. This kind of thinking was given a slightly different twist by one of our monks in a homily just before our last abbatial election. He said that anyone who desired to be abbot was obviously crazy, so he could not be elected.

All kidding aside, the question of ambition and suitability for monastic authority is quite serious. At one general chapter I remember an abbot commenting to the assembly that we seem to be locked into a difficult bind. Anyone who manifests any desire to be abbot is automatically disqualified by our ideology, if not our regulations; therefore those who do get elected can always protest that they never wanted to be abbot in the first place, all of which could lead to a serious lack of leadership in our communities.

One distinction that needs to be made is the difference between good and bad ambition. The first kind wants to dominate others; the second knows that the group needs leadership. If someone has that gift, she should be willing to exercise it. Granted, a selfish competition for power in a monastic community is a contradiction to the Gospel itself. But equally ruinous is the situation in which no one is willing to lead. It could be that they are all too humble, but it could be that none of them wants to sacrifice his precious career. For the abbacy is a very demanding job indeed.

Actually, the second part of RB 64 does address this question in an indirect way when it presents a series of qualifications for a good abbot. In general the abbot Benedict desires is anything but a power-player. He is a nonviolent personality along the lines of the Suffering Servant of Isaiah. Here is a representative quotation:

> When he must correct someone, he should act prudently and not overdo it. If he is too vigorous in removing the rust, he may break the vessel. Let him always be wary of his own brittleness, and remember not to break the bent reed . . . . He should aim more at being loved than feared. (RB 64.12-13, 15)

To speak directly to our point here, Benedict also gives us this wonderfully succinct aphorism: "He should realize that he must profit others rather than precede them." So there it is: true leadership is to profit others, not oneself. Anyone who hankers after such a role must either be selfless or a self-deluded fool.

Chapter Fourteen

The Prior of the Monastery

RB 65 on the Prior

In monastic language the prior is the second in command under the abbot. In the history of cenobitism communities of any size have usually had priors, simply for the reason that abbots found it useful and necessary to have a lieutenant who could stand in for them in their absence or share some of their duties when they were home. Surprisingly, St. Benedict does not seem to agree with this view of things.

Chapter 65 of his Rule, which is entirely devoted to the "Prior of the Monastery," is an almost shockingly negative diatribe against priors in general and certain priors in particular. Concerning priors in general he says: "There are some who become puffed up with an evil spirit of pride, thinking themselves second abbots and grasping at autonomous power. They nourish disputes and create quarrels in communities" (RB 65.2). As if this were not bad enough, he envisages an even more outrageous situation:

> This is particularly the danger in those places where the prior is installed by the same bishop or abbots who install the abbot. It is easy to see what an absurd arrangement this is, for from the very moment of installation the grounds for pride are present. His thoughts will suggest to him that he has been freed from the abbot's power. "You were installed by the same people who installed him!" (RB 65.3-6)

Further on in the chapter Benedict puts out a sort of general philosophical principle to explain why it is not a good idea to invest too much power in one person: "For when the management is entrusted to many, no one person will grow proud" (RB 65.13). On this basis Benedict says he would prefer to have several deans as his lieutenants rather than one prior.

Nevertheless, Benedict does appoint a prior for his monastery. He seems to do so against his better judgment, and even with a degree of bad grace. He makes it clear that the monks are pressing him to do so, but he warns them that they had better appeal to him "with good reason and humility" (RB 65.14). This implies that the author has felt the opposite, namely, a sort of mob pressure for a prior. But Benedict makes it plain that nobody is going to force him to appoint a prior he does not want: "(The abbot) himself should choose someone with the advice of God-fearing brothers, and make him *his* prior" (RB 65.15).

We could go on describing this chapter, but it is all along the same lines. It seems to me only someone with extreme devotion to St. Benedict could fail to see that he is not at his best in this chapter on the prior. What can we say to explain this strange and even embarrassing performance?

Some scholars suggest that the chapter was probably not written by St. Benedict. They note that there are no less than thirty-two *hapax legomena* in the vocabulary, that is, words used nowhere else in the Rule. Some feel that an author as mild-mannered and benevolent as Benedict would hardly inflict this harsh diatribe on his followers. In answer to that, I would point to RB 46.1-4 and 71.6-9 as passages that betray the same ferocious tone. No, Benedict was not always under complete self-control—which reassures me that he was no plaster saint but flesh and blood like the rest of us.

Another, more convincing explanation of this puzzling chapter points out that there is another chapter of the Rule that shows some influence from RB 65 but indicates a more satisfactory solution to the question of the sharing of authority in the monastery. RB 65.14-15, quoted above, shares much vocabulary with RB 3.11, indeed, so much that one must influence the other. Borias thinks that RB 3 represents Benedict's more mature thinking on these issues. By creating a permanent "small council" of elders he ensures a constant flow of communication from the community. This could have spared him the unpleasant situation that disfigures RB 65.

An interesting and highly significant historical insight on RB 65 is supplied by a study of early papal correspondence. The very situation Benedict so thoroughly abhors, namely, the same outside person appointing both the abbot and the prior, in fact turns up twice in the official letters of Pope Gregory I. In *Letters* 5.6 and 11.48 that eminent churchman has no qualms about installing both the abbot and prior in two monasteries. There may be some question about whether Gregory had actually read the Rule of

Benedict, but there can be no doubt that he thought it was proper for him as pope to appoint both monastic officials.

In addition to this fascinating detail from church history it should also be noted that such situations cannot have been that unusual in the course of monastic history. From what we know, priors were a standard feature in most medieval monasteries. It is also well known that there was a good deal of outside interference in monasteries throughout Europe. Probably it was unusual for a pope to intervene in monastic affairs, but certainly it was not thus with bishops and kings and other potentates. In fact, the arrangement presented as normative by the Rule, that is, that the abbot be elected by the monks and then himself choose the rest of the monastic officials, was very often violated in feudal Europe.

Furthermore, what are we to think about RB 64? In that chapter, which comes just before the embattled chapter on the prior, we read the following:

> But it can happen that a whole community may conspire to choose a person who will go along with their vices—may it never happen! If those goings-on somehow come to the notice of the local diocesan bishop, or to the abbots or Christians of the district, they must block the evildoers from succeeding in their scheme. They should instead set a worthy steward over the house of God. And they may be sure that they will receive a good reward for this deed if they have done it out of pure motives and godly zeal. But if they neglect their duty, they will be punished. (RB 64.3-6)

This passage is interesting, but it is not in very close accord with RB 65! After inviting the neighbors to appoint a good abbot if the monks cannot manage to do it themselves, Benedict then rages and fumes when someone *does* intervene to appoint a prior.

Another aspect of the Rule of Benedict that has to be kept in mind through all his opposition to a prior is the simple fact that he himself is very committed to the hierarchical system (RB 63). This means that all the monks have a rank in comparison to one another. The abbot, of course, ranks first, but inevitably someone else ranks second and third to him. Whether this person be called "prior" or something else, or whether or not he has special authority, he will still have some kind of status that has to be taken into consideration. Otherwise the chaotic situation created by the Rule of the Master will ensue. We will speak of that next.

Finally, in trying to come to some kind of objective evaluation of Benedict's chapter on the prior we have to admit that in itself it is the farthest thing from objective. This chapter is loaded with inflammatory language, and it does not take a very sharp psychologist to see that something is very wrong here. It is clear, to me at least, that this chapter bespeaks a bitter experience for Benedict. When he wrote about it he had still not calmed down sufficiently to do the topic of the prior justice. A good editor might have urged him to take another run at the subject when the pain had subsided.

The Rule of the Master

Although there is no literary evidence that Benedict was influenced on this question by the Rule of the Master, it is still worth casting a glance at that earlier Rule. What does the Master say about the prior? He has essentially the same view of the office as Benedict: "The abbot must take care never to appoint anyone second to himself, nor to assign anyone to third place." The Master worries about the same thing as Benedict, namely, that the second (prior, *praepositus*) would become proud and usurp privilege to himself. But unlike Benedict, the Master carries this theory into practice: he refuses to appoint a prior. What then? Like Benedict, he has a system of deans, but it must be said that these deans have no real authority: more about that later.

After very candidly expressing his fears about ambition in his subordinates the Master spends two very long and excruciatingly boring chapters, RM 92–93, devising a system of the transfer of authority in his monastery. To put it bluntly, he creates a kind of monastic proletariat in which nobody except the abbot has any rank or authority. He thinks he has a very good reason for doing that: so that all may aspire to become the next abbot! He proposes a dynastic system in which the abbot keeps a sharp lookout for the most obedient and humble brother. When the abbot approaches death, voilà, he names this brother his successor!

Probably the reader will already have sensed that there are large problems lurking in such an arrangement. For example, what is to prevent hypocrisy? The Master urges the monks to *look humble* in front of the abbot so he will be chosen the humblest. Another anomaly occurs when it dawns on the Master that the old abbot may not in fact die after he has named his successor. If that happens, the one designated is indeed in a jam since the abbot is then to watch him like a hawk. If he shows the slightest sign of arrogance at his prospect as the next leader he is to be deposed and put in the lowest place.

The whole crazy system is painful to describe, and some authors would even doubt whether Benedict ever saw this part of the Rule of the Master. I am quite sure he did, and that he wanted no part of it. Since it is plainly the product of a paranoid and twisted mind, someone with the good sense of Benedict would find it alien. Still, Benedict is not himself entirely devoid of a certain amount of fear in regard to his subordinate officials. Some of that was probably a symptom of the time. The sixth century was not an age of shared authority.

André Girard on Mimesis

Without plunging fully into his whole system of thought, it may be good to at least mention the thinking of André Girard, the French philosopher who taught for years in the United States. Girard's main research revolved around the problem of human conflict. Why are people at each other's throats so often? There are a lot of possible answers to that, including the Catholic doctrine of original sin. Girard is a believing Catholic, but he is not quite satisfied with such an answer—or at least he thinks we can learn something from analyzing it.

Girard thinks that something he calls *mimesis* lies at the heart of much human violence. To put it plainly, he thinks people come into conflict because they want the same thing other people want. Indeed, he says they only learn *what* to want by looking at other people. If they have it, we want it! And since this kind of rivalry is based on a kind of zero-sum thinking that posits a scarcity of goods, it is sure to create discord and violence. There is a lot more to Girard's theory, but even at this point we might wonder how it could apply to monastic authority.

Why should anyone aspire to monastic leadership? Aside from the fact that some people have a natural aptitude to lead others, there is a basic consideration that would seem to rule out any monastic rivalry. As Benedict teaches us at great length in RB 7, the hallmark of the good monk should be *humility*. Although he never directly says in that extremely detailed chapter that the humble monk should never aspire to leadership, that conclusion could easily be deduced. This could result in a situation that is rarely ever mentioned in monastic literature, namely, that *nobody* is able or willing to lead the community. In recent times some monastic elections have been aborted for exactly that reason.

It could be that these questions regarding authority depend on the "spirit of the age." Anyone who reads monastic history from the earlier period of American monasticism might get the impression that people on the frontier were a different breed than we are today. The early histories of our communities are often marked by fairly sharp conflicts over various issues, and it does not seem that the participants (maybe we could call them the *belligerents*) were particularly shy in pursuing what they thought was best. Nowadays chapter meetings are comparatively tame, and I think it is because *we* are comparatively tame.

Getting back to Girard, I do not remember if he ever discusses the difference between envy and jealousy. It seems to me he mostly deals with envy, that is, a situation in which someone wants what someone else has. But what about the other vice, that is, jealousy? Now the shoe is on the other foot, for I do not want what you have; rather, I am afraid that you will take away what is mine. At the risk of seeming churlish, is this not what we have with Benedict's chapter on the prior? He seems desperately afraid that his assistant will somehow usurp his power and authority. In other words, he is jealous of his prior.

I have already come in for some negative criticism for my commentary on RB 65 in my book, *Benedict's Rule*, and I can well imagine that this talk of abbatial jealousy will add fuel to the fire. But sometimes it does help to call things by their right name, and I think the right name here is jealousy. The most benign interpretation I can give to it here is that for some reason Benedict's own sense of his authority was shaky, for a truly strong authority does not spend its time agonizing over the possible insubordination of its collaborators.

It seems to me that even a cursory reading of history and biography shows us the fruits of jealousy. Is it not characteristic of tyrants of every stripe that they cannot tolerate real authority when it appears in their subordinates? Granted, only the most vicious regimes systematically destroy secondary leaders as soon as they display competence, but this danger lurks in every leader who is insecure in his own authority. No one likes to associate St. Benedict with perverted and homicidal leaders who are motivated mostly by paranoia, but RB 65 does seem to fit into that category.

Delegation

Another concept we should probably invoke at this late point in our discussion is *delegation*. In this case I take it to mean the conferral of authority on another person to act in my name. Notice that this is not just a matter of naming the other one to a certain office. Such titles are empty and worse than nothing if they carry no real authority with them. Delegation means that the subordinate official is given real power to act with true authority. It does not mean that such a one is therefore autonomous, but it does mean he is *trusted*. To claim to delegate authority but then neglect to back up that person with confidence is a cruel hoax. It is the hallmark of both dictators and weak authorities down through history.

Does St. Benedict understand these things? Not to judge from RB 65! But other significant passages in the Rule would indicate he almost certainly does. Here is what he says about the deans, an office he likes much better than prior:

> If the community is large, let there be chosen from them brothers of good reputation and holy life, and let these be made deans. In all matters they should take care of their deaneries according to commandments of God and the orders of their abbot. Only those should be chosen deans with whom the abbot can confidently share his burdens. They should not be chosen by rank, but by the merit of their lives and the wisdom of their teaching. (RB 21.1-3)

In these few lines we can sense a serene and confident authority that is ready and willing to seek out competent and wise people in the community with whom to share leadership. These are not just functionaries who merely carry out mechanical tasks, nor are they mere watchdogs such as we find with the deans in the Rule of the Master (RM 11). Here it is a question of people of quality who are chosen for true spiritual leadership. Otherwise why require that they be holy and of good reputation? Moreover, they are expected to possess their own wise teaching. In other words, they are not just clones of the abbot who simply parrot his teaching.

This is not the only place where Benedict bestows genuine delegated authority on his lower officials. In the chapters on the cellarer (31), the novice master (58), and the "spiritual seniors" (46.5-6) one gets the same impression that delegation actually takes place. The contrast with the Rule of the Master could not be sharper. Nobody in that Rule has any authority except the abbot. Indeed, the Master often demands that everybody be kept in a condition of complete subordination to prevent pride or ambition from breaking out. Of course, such a thing can happen in the best of circumstances, wherever monks are marked by the sin of our first parents. But abuse should not take away use: delegation is still necessary.

Before we credit Benedict with too much benevolence in regard to delegation, however, it is only honest to add that he almost always makes sure to hedge this delegation with threats against those who abuse it. For example, RB 31 grants a good deal of authority, both temporal and spiritual, to the cellarer. But every other verse is devoted to warning the cellarer not to abuse his office! He is told over and over again that the abbot is the real master of the community and he (the cellarer) is not. Yet it could be pointed out that the abbot himself is given the same treatment in RB 2, where the author alternates between bestowal of huge authority and threats of what kind of judgment will await its abuse.

At this point I would like to put in a good word for all subordinate monastic officials. I think it is worth considering briefly the position in which they find themselves. They do not appoint themselves; they are put in place by the abbot, and by him alone. As collaborators of the abbot they have serious duties to perform that again are largely defined by the abbot. I might add here that the office of prior is notoriously open-ended. Notice that the Rule itself says almost nothing about the prior's actual purview. Thus some priors are given a great deal of discretion by their abbot, and some are not. Some abbots want and need a good deal of help, and some can run things by themselves. So the prior may be almost anything, big or small.

Still, the prior is like any other monastic official. He has a role to play, but it is definitely subordinate. That means he is essentially a person who must carry out the abbot's wishes. If he does not, he will not be a loyal assistant. But it also means that he often does not have a decisive hand in shaping policy. Of course, most people in the secular work world are in the same position: they have to work within parameters set by someone else. At any rate, I think monastic officials at least deserve the respect due to someone who carries out a limited but responsible task. The "buck does not stop with him," but he is still responsible.

One of the reasons why I am not happy with RB 65 is that I do not feel it is fair to the prior, whoever he may be. When we look for something positive in this chapter, what do we find? Little or nothing. Surely the second in command deserves *some* encouragement for a role that is always rather delicate, even if it is not always too onerous. The suggestion that priors are power-hungry ingrates who cannot be trusted is blatantly unfair to hundreds and thousands of good and loyal men. They did not and do not have the pressure of ultimate responsibility hanging around their necks, but they are still very important to the well-being of the community.

Most of us who have lived long years in a community are aware that the prior is often a very useful complement to the abbot. Not every abbot can be all things to all persons, but with the help of a good prior (or subprioress for monastic women) he can provide a fuller form of leadership by choosing good lieutenants. I am not one of those who wishes to have this or that chapter expunged from the Rule. All of it gives us a better-balanced picture of the author. But RB 65 does suggest that, at least now and then, the emperor has no clothes.

Chapter Fifteen *Zeal, Bad and Good*

An Abundance of Anger

One of the most notable and distressing aspects of contemporary life on planet earth is the abundance of anger. Wherever you look or listen someone is ranting and raving, or perhaps blowing himself and other people to smithereens. Now of course anger is a basic passion of the human psyche, so it cannot be all bad. We need it to cope with the evil in the world. But disordered anger is a problem serious enough to be classified as one of the seven capital sins. So anger has always been around, but for some reason it seems to have metastasized in our world.

No doubt one of the reasons anger has become so prominent among us is that it has found some very useful outlets for itself. One of them is what we call "talk radio," which means almost all radio today. Turn on your radio and what do you hear? Somebody bellowing uncontrollably about some pet peeve of his. These loudmouths now fill up much of the airwaves; they are paid untold millions to shout at us for hour after hour. And apparently there are enough people who listen to them that the sponsors keep them on the air.

Another form of the same thing can be found in "call-in radio," which flourishes especially in the middle of the night. Now the cranks and the fanatics can call in to expatiate on their favorite hobby-horse. Occasionally the talk-show host will interrupt them to correct this or that egregious mistake of fact, but by and large they are allowed to blab on and on. This has the effect of attracting other crazies, who then call in and add their two cents. Of course some of this is harmless gossip about sports, but some of it is bloodcurdling nonsense about politics and culture. Since this is a free country, hate speech is generally given quite a bit of room to operate.

A third form of broadcast anger occurs with the television roundtables. These are more respectable in appearance, usually featuring educated panelists discussing serious subjects. But the usual format is to bring together volatile combinations of angry partisans whom the moderators goad into shouting matches. For some reason this now passes for rational discussion, but it really does not follow the rules of civilized conversation. Everybody is shouting and nobody is listening.

Internet chatrooms and blogs are another place where a good deal of anger gets vented. Of course, this medium is cooler than radio or TV, but that doesn't mean the fury is any less. Indeed, since it is not necessary to sign your name to these statements it is a perfect place to express the most extreme, outrageous points of view, things one would normally be ashamed to express. Usually this kind of venting is the sign of a fanatic whom people steer clear of. Such cranks usually end up isolated and lonely, but now they can find an outlet, and even some companionship on these blogs.

Angry Idealism

Still, it would not be right to condemn all angry expression since much of it is aimed at a good cause. After all, there are terrible things in this world that need to be opposed, and it takes special energy to do it. Yet such energy, which we can label *zeal*, is dangerous stuff and can quite easily get out of hand. One of the occupational hazards for people who oppose evil is to slip over the line into fanaticism. They can become radicalized for a worthy cause. For whatever reasons the cause takes over their minds and their lives to the point that they cannot think or talk of anything else. They become difficult to live with and even antisocial.

We all have some experience with cranks. They are typically humorless people, unable to see anything funny about the situation, and especially unable to laugh at themselves. They also lose any ability to see any good in the cause or the people they are opposing. Of course when they arrive at that point they cannot tolerate any questioning of their own position. They are completely right, and anybody who points out some of the complexities of the situation is immediately dismissed as a dupe, a fool, and even worse. In fact, you cannot please a fanatic except by joining him in his obsession.

Needless to say, such people are a divisive element in the ordinary community. While they may be able to form a coterie with those who share their obsession they are much less at home in the larger community. Society is made up of all sorts of people with different mentalities, but a fanatic cannot be satisfied unless he has managed to polarize the group. The only configuration he understands is "us versus them," and the only question in his mind is whether you are for him or against him. Any kind of neutrality is out of the question. It is flabby relativism and is deemed intolerable.

As I have hinted above, one of the chief difficulties with fanaticism is its tendency to "suck all the air out of the room." By that I mean that no other consideration is of any interest to the zealot; he considers any other issue but his own to be beside the point. But the inconvenient fact is that there are many important issues that are worthy of our serious consideration. To allow someone or some group to reduce the entire moral menu to one supreme concern is to neglect everything else. But the fanatic cannot keep more than one question on his front burner, so this kind of concern escapes him. He needs to focus all his energy on one problem, so don't bother him with distractions.

Another characteristic of the fanatic that I find particularly disastrous at the present time is his need for direct attack on the problem as he sees it. Of course there is something very satisfying about such a tactic. You identify the target and you destroy it. It is a kind of military approach to life. The trouble is that some problems, indeed *many* problems, cannot be solved in that fashion. Why? because they simply won't stand still. Perhaps they are so subtle or many-sided that they always slip away from us. But if we insist on a frontal attack we may just be worsening the problem.

Anybody reading this attack on fanaticism has no difficulty conjuring up some examples. All of us are irritated by certain contemporary crusades and their partisans. Let me name a few: radical environmentalism, radical feminism, radical anti-abortion crusading, radical pacifism, radical patriotism. Maybe I haven't named your favorite *bête noire*, so you can fill in the blanks. Note well, please, that I am not discounting any of these movements as such, just their radical forms.

No doubt one of the most worrisome forms of modern fanaticism is international terrorism. It has all the earmarks of fanaticism, but in this case people have found ways to give it truly spectacular forms of expression. The current favorite is suicide bombing, where someone is so convulsed with the need to attack society that he is willing to destroy himself in the process. Fanaticism can hardly go much further than that.

Here again, contemporary technological culture provides the means to implement the hatred. Without the aid of modern explosives, and even jet-liners on 9/11, the fanatic could not bring off his wild attack. And this is very appropriate in his mind because he really is attacking the "system" of modern life, including its technology. He is willing to use the most diabolically clever techniques in order to get back at the technological society as such. Instead of ranting on a talk show or a blog, this kind of fanatic puts words into action, and he is partially successful in his crazy mission because he has succeeded in casting a spell of fear over the whole civilized world.

Some people feel that the roots of this kind of fanaticism are essentially religious. In fact, the Islamicist bombers wrap themselves in the Qu'ran and justify themselves by some of its verses. But I think the deeper causes here are primarily socio-economic. Surely it cannot be a mere accident that all the terrorists on the 9/11 planes were young men with good scientific educations obtained in the West. But what all of them also had in common was a serious lack of anything to do with that training. Since the Middle East has no real place for educated and trained young people, they faced a dead end. So they struck back in rage at the West that has educated them for such frustration.

There is also a general feeling among some people in the Middle East that the West is corrupt and must be defeated or destroyed. They feel they cannot ignore the problem because Western culture tends to permeate the minds of people all over the globe. No matter how backward or primitive the country, its children still find a way to listen to American songs and watch American videos. Since the values we communicate are basically an amoral materialism that threatens traditional tenets and especially religious values, they try to fight back with radical, fanatical forms of Islam. But of course American culture is another one of those targets that will not stand still for direct attack.

Benedict's View of Anger

Saint Benedict does not have a separate treatise on anger, but he has a memorable statement about it in the final, climactic chapter of his Rule: "Just as there is an evil and bitter zeal that separates one from God and leads to hell, so too there is a good zeal that separates one from evil and leads to God and eternal life" (RB 72.1-2).

The first thing we notice about this rather formal, almost classical pronouncement is that Benedict uses the unusual term *zeal* to make his point. What precisely is zeal? In my commentary on RB 72 I defined it as "exceptional fervor and enthusiasm for an object." As such it is a neutral force, available for good or bad use. It has this same meaning in Greek, Latin, and English. But in English most of the usages of the root *zelus* are negative. Thus when we call somebody a zealot we mean he is a fanatic. And of course jealousy is a vice that sometimes leads to murder.

Benedict's phrase "evil zeal of bitterness" is particularly pungent, and it probably comes from James 3:14-17, which reads:

> But if you have bitter jealousy and selfish ambition in your hearts, do not boast and be false to the truth. Wisdom of this kind does not come down from above but is earthly, unspiritual, demonic. For where jealousy and selfish ambition exist, there is disorder and every foul practice. But the wisdom from above is first of all pure, then peaceable, gentle, compliant, full of mercy and good fruits, without inconstancy or insincerity. (NABRE)

We can hear a lot of Benedict's own language in this passage. For example, both authors talk about heaven and hell. But whereas Benedict says bad zeal leads to hell, James says it comes from hell. It must come from hell, he says, because it produces such terrible consequences: disorder and every foul practice.

Another early text that mentions bad zeal is the letter of Clement of Rome to the church of Corinth (*1 Clement 9*). For whatever reasons, the Greek clergy have deposed their bishop. That won't do, says Clement. It is bad zeal and it must stop! Furthermore, their bad zeal must be replaced with good zeal. Specifically this means they must reinstate the bishop. But in my view the interesting point here is that Clement does not think the remedy for bad zeal is *no zeal*. In his opinion the answer must lie in the direction of good zeal.

Benedict seems to think along the same lines because he is very careful to balance bad zeal with good zeal. And he, like James, thinks of good zeal in very exalted terms. Whereas James says it comes "from above," that is, from God, Benedict says that good zeal "leads to God and eternal life." So it is clear that Benedict sees the question of bad and good zeal as a stark choice admitting of no neutrality. Unlike many modern commentators, these ancient authors do not see the antidote to modern fanaticism in cool, secular objectivity. The Bible and Benedict know better. They believe one must choose to be all for God or all against Him.

But what exactly is this evil zeal Benedict wants to replace with good zeal? I have been describing it here as anger, but he does not do that in RB 72. Rather, he prefers to describe good zeal and then let us infer what bad zeal is from that. So what is good zeal? According to RB 72.3 and the rest of this chapter, the answer is love: "Thus monks should practice this zeal with the warmest love." This sentence can also be construed to mean that good zeal *is* in fact love, and not just any love but the *warmest* love: *ferventissimo amore*.

Let me linger a moment on that adjective *ferventissimo*. It is what we call a superlative, the highest degree of a certain quality. I am surprised at the way some translations (such as *RB 1980*, p. 295) render it simply "fervent love."

Maybe it seemed to them that we have here one of those false superlatives that really do not mean to be taken too seriously. Perhaps they felt Benedict was a typical Italian, tempted to go overboard at times with his rhetoric. To that I would reply that he was a sober Roman, not given to excess.

Still, if we read on in RB 72 we might wonder if Benedict is so sober and realistic. Listen to this summary: 4. Respect other people. 5. Very patiently bear each other's weaknesses of body and character. 6. Compete with one another in obedience. 7. Prefer the interest of others to your own. 8. Show selfless love to the brother.

Let me expand a bit on two of those verses. What does it mean to bear one another's burdens of body and spirit with the greatest patience? First of all, notice again that superlative: "the greatest patience." Patience is not a virtue that is very attractive to the modern sensibility. It does not mesh very well with many aspects of contemporary life. Patience takes time, often a long time; we like to do things in a hurry. If you have a computer that takes five seconds to perform some function, you seethe. Above all we want instant gratification.

The difficulty here is that many problems are not quickly solvable. We know very well that many physical difficulties require long-term treatment, and when it comes to weaknesses of character we enter a realm of slower, even glacial change. When we are asked to bear the weaknesses of others out of love, we know there is no guarantee at all that they will or even can change. And in our better moments we know full well that unless others do the same for us we have no place in community. Patience is simply the price to be paid for human society.

The second verse I would lift up for examination is this one: "No one should pursue what he judges advantageous to himself, but rather what benefits others." If we are honest we probably find this saying almost unbearable. Doesn't Benedict know that we humans are basically motivated by self-interest? He knows very well that this is our tendency as the result of original sin, but it is still not an adequate Christian ethic. To be a disciple of Christ is to transcend self-interest in the same fashion the Master himself did. He lived for others, and he also died for others.

Someone who is biblically literate might be aware that this verse comes from a section of Paul's letter to the Philippians in which he wants to ground Christian behavior on the model of Christ. He tells the Philippians they must live selflessly and take on this other-centered mentality precisely because of the example of Christ:

> Who though he was in the form of God, did not count equality with God a thing to be grasped, but emptied himself, taking the form of a servant,

being born in the likeness of men. And being found in human form he humbled himself and became obedient unto death, even death on a cross. (Phil 2:4-8, RSV)

Someone might be justified in asking whether Benedict actually put this extremely demanding ethic of love, which he calls "good zeal," into practice. Rather than examining his *Life* as told by St. Gregory the Great, I would prefer simply to point to a few significant chapters in his Rule. In RB 27 he urges the abbot to be "preoccupied" with the troubled brother and do everything to reconcile him to the community. In RB 31 the cellarer is admonished to treat all the monks in a fatherly way, even the brother who is demanding and unreasonable. In RB 36 the infirmarian is to told to deal with the sick as with Christ himself. And the guests and the knockers on the door are also to be treated with Christlike hospitality.

To return to bad zeal, the primary focus of this chapter, if we want to know what it is we just have to think of the mirror opposite of these attitudes promulgated in RB 72. The fanatic does not respect the person (72.4) of his opponent because he cares only about pushing across his agenda. He has no patience for the weaknesses of others (72.5), and especially for what he sees as their muddled ideas, because he feels the time is short and he must solve the problem ruthlessly. As for mutual obedience (72.6), that means at least listening to what others have to say, and he has no time for that either. Nor can he see much use in putting the interests of others before his own, for he is right and they are wrong. In short, RB 72 is an unbearable philosophy for the zealot. Nevertheless, it is not as alien to him as it is to the secularist or the materialist. For them it is based on a totally absurd view of what matters in this world. The zealot, however, can at least respect the spiritual energy, the zeal operative in RB 72. All he needs to do now is substitute the good zeal for his bad zeal.

Chapter Sixteen   *Hierarchy*

In the Rule of Benedict there is a curious chapter given over exclusively to the question of hierarchy in the monastery. RB 63 on "rank in the community" is hardly one of the favorite chapters of most nuns and monks in our time, and yet it cannot be denied that Benedict thought it important, since he has devoted no fewer than nineteen verses to the subject.

For those who have not read it or perhaps have forgotten it, RB 63 determines the rank of the monks by a very simple system, namely, time of entry into the community. This means the one who comes at the first hour is ahead of the one who comes at the second hour (v. 8). Thus the time of arrival determines who is *senior* and who is *junior*. Right away we can sense a source of confusion, can we not? What if the person coming earlier is actually much younger than the one who comes next? No matter, says Benedict, this system does not depend on "age or status."

A careful reader of RB 63 will notice that I have deliberately elided a few details in this system. In fact, Benedict mentions two other factors that are to be taken into account in establishing the communal order. In addition to date of entry, "merit of life or the abbot's arrangement" are also to be acknowledged. Since the assessment of merit also looks to the abbot we might say that Benedict expects the abbot to fine-tune the basic arrangement. Apparently he finds time of entry to be an insufficient criterion that needs to be seasoned with wisdom and discernment.

One of the elements that makes RB 63 somewhat less than attractive is what we might term its didacticism. Although the system seems to be quite straightforward—indeed, that is part of its effectiveness—Benedict still thinks he must spell it out in detail. "Therefore the brothers should approach for the kiss of peace and for Holy Communion, to intone a psalm and to stand in choir, according to the rank the abbot has given them or which they themselves have." This kind of focus on details may be the result of influence by an earlier Rule, namely, that of Pachomius (Pref. 3). But it may also indicate a certain amount of tension brought on by conflict.

Although this is not the kind of argument that can be scientifically proven, it is well to be aware of these kinds of considerations when reading an ancient text. Why is the author insisting so adamantly? Is he reacting against something? Can we perhaps discover what it might be? In fact, good scholars like André Borias have studied the Rule with a special eye toward noting just such "hot spots." They even suggest that one can construct a sort of history of the composition of the text based on such stress points. Again, what might Benedict be reacting against here?

If we note the position of RB 63 within the framework of the Rule we see that it immediately precedes a chapter on the election of the abbot. That being the case, we might then expect that the author will suggest the senior by rank should naturally be elected to the top post. But that is not at all what is said. Instead, we read: "Let the candidate be chosen for merit of life and wisdom of teaching, even if he hold the last rank in the community" (RB 64.2). This seems to complicate things a bit, does it not? After carefully establishing the communal *ordo* by date of entry, thus setting aside the traditional factors of age and status, Benedict now shows that rank, too, is not everything when it comes to the practical ordering of the community.

Although the juxtaposition of RB 63 and RB 64 does not establish a clear relationship of influence, both chapters reject the traditional basis of authority in ordinary society. Because we live today in a rather nontraditional society we may find it hard to feel the full impact of this "revolution" on the part of Benedict (and in fact all the early monastic authors). When they rejected mere age, and especially social status, as the basis for authority in the monastic community they were in fact going against the whole grain of ancient wisdom.

In that society age and years of experience were very much respected as the basis of leadership, or at least of wisdom. It was taken for granted that those who have lived longest have accumulated the most wisdom and therefore should be deferred to. So the oldest man spoke first and then the next eldest and so forth. In our own time this kind of thinking is generally considered obsolete because so much of our knowledge comes through science, which depends not on experience but on expertise. Nowadays grandma needs the five-year-old child to program her alarm clock.

Of course when Benedict rejects age he does not do so for scientific reasons. He does it because he knows that the monastic community is based on the life of the Spirit, and the Spirit is not limited by spatio-temporal considerations. Consequently, if the Spirit is seen to be most alive in the brother or sister who is last in rank (because of recent entry), then that one should be placed over the community. The Spirit is not boxed in by date of entry. The canon law of the Catholic Church, however, imposes its own restrictions on this and requires that a monk be in final vows seven years before he can be elected.

But there is another possible factor that may enter into Benedict's thinking when he sets up his monastic *ordo* in RB 63. It is well known today that Benedict was heavily influenced by an Italian monastic rule that was written shortly before his own. This is the *Rule of the Master*, which was almost unknown throughout monastic history until a few years ago. What does the Master have to say about the election of an abbot? What does he have to say about rank in the community?

Taking up the last point first, we can report that the Master has nothing at all to say about rank in the community. There is simply no parallel chapter to RB 63 in the Rule of the Master. Is it possible that there was no hierarchy among his monks? Yes, it is. In fact, a close inspection of the entire document shows that in the eyes of the Master the monks are all perfectly equal. There is no mention of seniors and juniors because date of entry means nothing. Furthermore, there is virtually no differentiation among the brothers. All depend entirely on the abbot, and relations among the community count for very little. To put it as plainly as possible, all of the Master's monks are treated the same—like dogs.

If that sounds like a crass exaggeration, then consider a somewhat offhand comment of the author in his chapter on the "kinds of monks": "Therefore all who still have folly as their mother ought to be subject to the authority of a superior so that, guided on their way by the judgment of a teacher, they may learn to avoid the way of self-will." In addition to this incredibly pessimistic view of the ordinary "monk in the trenches," the Master makes the serious category mistake of locating the abbot on a level with the bishop in terms of church authority.

In general, the master-disciple tradition that began with the Egyptian desert and continued through at least Cassian and the Master tends to emphasize the differences between persons. This takes the form of an insistence that one Christian subordinate himself to another, more spiritually advanced spiritual master. As a general program for vigorous spiritual striving it is not bad advice, but when it is pressed too hard it tends to exaggerate the spiritual gifts of a few special souls and undervalue the maturity of ordinary people. In fact, many monks and nuns report that they receive their best spiritual direction unbidden from their brothers and sisters.

To return to the Rule of the Master, its extremely pessimistic anthropology has all kinds of baleful effects, and one of these has to do with the transmission of authority in the monastery. Unlike Benedict, the Master has no election for abbot; rather, he promotes a dynastic succession with the abbot choosing his own successor. This in itself need not always be a bad thing, but in the Master's case it is disastrous. In order to choose the worthy successor the abbot is advised to keep a sharp lookout for the humblest and most obedient of his subjects. For their part, the Master urges the monks to *look good in front of the abbot* (RM 92) so as to be chosen the new abbot!

Along with this ludicrous abbatial beauty contest, the Master insists that no one in the monastery (except the abbot) should have any rank at all. That will serve at least two purposes. First, it will keep individuals from getting too proud as a result of their prestige or status. Second, it will keep everyone from getting complacent. If they have no status they will all remain hungry for the ultimate prize, namely, the abbacy. But why go on with this utterly bizarre scenario? I suggest that Benedict carefully avoids anything resembling this recipe for community envy and jealousy by simply assigning each monk a rank and letting the chips fall where they may.

Contemporary Egalitarianism

When the present author entered the monastery some fifty years ago rank was very evident at every level of Benedictine life. We marched *in statio*, received communion *in statio*, sat at table in order of rank, our choir stalls were assigned strictly according to date of profession, and on and on. This was one of those items from the Rule of Benedict that was taken quite literally. Everybody knew who was his senior and who was his junior; the monastic *ordo* was reinforced by our everyday praxis.

This system was brought home to me very graphically when I first came to the novitiate. There were only two of us, and we were informed that I was the junior and my confrère was the senior. How was that determined? Since we were both classmates from the Abbey school who had been together for six years in every aspect of school life we wondered how they chose the senior? It was explained that my classmate had registered a few hours before I did on a September day some six years previously. We laughed at this strange custom, but I stopped laughing when I learned that the novice master would only deal with the senior novice when it came to group permissions and so on. And this went on all year long.

Not all novice masters were such imbeciles. At St. John's Abbey in the 1920s there was a class of twenty novices. On the first day Br. Michael was informed that he was senior, and he made sure everybody was kept well aware of his exalted status for the next couple of weeks. Then one day the novice master said to Mike: "Oh, I forgot to mention that this is a rotation system. So now you go to the end of the *statio* until your turn comes up again in four months!" Of course that also meant the group had four months to put poor Mike back in his place. I don't suppose the novice master got his idea from the Rule of the Master, since nobody had ever read that Rule in 1924. But he obviously had a good appreciation of the democratic notion of egalitarianism.

As it turns out, the Benedictine custom of hierarchical relations has mostly disappeared in the past fifty years. After the Second Vatican Council and the far-reaching effects it had on all aspects of monastic life most monastic communities deemphasized hierarchy among their members. Although some aspects of the system remain in most communities one rarely sees rank carried out to the extent it once was. For example, many communities now observe random seating at table or they eat at round tables where rank is not obvious. In choir some communities arrange the monks in such a way as to promote a good balance of singing voices. And it would be a very rare community that would now have its members approach for Holy Communion by rank.

When I say all of this was a result of Vatican II, I cannot point to any one council document that requests or demands a de-emphasis of hierarchy among the monks. Even though Rome did promote certain equalizing measures such as a unified system of formation resulting in solemn vows for all members (including brothers), the influence was mostly indirect. Probably one could say the overall thrust of the council was to work toward a downgrading of distinction and rank in the Christian body. A perfect symbol of that aim can be seen in the typical form taken by the current monastic eucharistic ritual. In most monasteries the monks all stand in a circle around the altar. Some may wear albs because they are priests, but all stand on the same level and face in the same direction—the center, which is Christ.

It would not be entirely honest to gloss over the fact that now, fifty years after the council, some people are not happy with this "new" equalization. One suspects that one of the underlying motives of the push for a return to the Tridentine Mass is precisely its hierarchical symbolism. In the traditional rite the priest faced God, with his back to the people, who also faced God. The priest was at their head, not on an equal footing with them. The whole notion of the People of God together praying the Eucharist was not obvious. The priest was the intermediary between humanity and God. As such he held a rank above the common faithful.

How does all of this look in the light of church history? What does the New Testament have to say about the question? By and large, hierarchical rank has very little place in the gospels and epistles. The very terms hardly occur, much less any detailed discussion of rank among the disciples of Jesus. In fact, it is not hard to find passages that positively undercut rank as something that Christians should even care about. A passage like the following says it all:

> And they came to Capernaum; and when he was in the house he asked them, "What were you discussing on the way?" But they were silent; for on the way they had discussed with one another who was the greatest. Then he sat down and called the twelve; and he said to them, "If any one would be the first, he must be last of all and servant of all. (Mark 9:33-35, RSV)

The same kind of equality in Christ is sometimes expressed by Jesus' use of the term "brother" (*adelphos*) in his discourse. When his family comes to see him, Jesus states flatly: "Here are my mother and my brothers. For whoever does the will of God is my brother and sister and mother" (Mark 3:34, RSV).

If we pause to ponder a little on this term "brother" in regard to our subject here, namely, hierarchy, we can see at once that it does not fit the pattern. The term "brother" in itself implies no superiority or subordination. As such, all brothers are equal. It is a horizontal term, not a vertical one. And even apart from the familial context, brotherhood implies common membership in a covenant bond with deep ramifications. As soon as you call someone brother (or sister) you thereby admit that they have a claim on your sustenance and protection. To put it in current jargon, it means you "have their back."

To approach the question of ancient hierarchy from a different direction, it has been said that society at the time of Jesus was absolutely saturated with it. In the Greco-Roman world everyone belonged to someone else. Either you were the powerful one, the patron, or you were the client, that is, someone dependent on the patron. I do not know if this social arrangement was prevalent in Palestine, but it was an overwhelming fact of life in the rest of the Mediterranean world. Therefore it is quite significant that the most prominent early missionary of the Gospel, namely, Paul of Tarsus, was distinguished by his categorical rejection of the whole idea of patronage. To put it bluntly, Paul denied that he was a client of anyone but his Lord and Master, Jesus Christ.

According to John Dominic Crossan (*In Search of Paul*), this was what made him such a dangerous man in the eyes of the Roman authorities. Although Luke in Acts makes it appear that the Romans really did not want to execute Paul because they didn't have much of a case against him, Crossan thinks they were more than happy to have him out of the way. And this is not too hard to imagine if we remember certain sayings of Paul such as "for as many of you as were baptized into Christ have put on Christ. There is neither Jew nor Greek, there is neither slave nor free, there is neither male nor female; for you are all one in Christ Jesus" (Gal 3:27-28, RSV).

Still, it is well to remember that this kind of revolutionary talk did not result in an upheaval of ordinary life. Even though Paul rejected the distinction between masters and slaves "in Christ," he did not then urge the slaves to revolt. Moreover, he recommends that wives remain subordinate to their husbands and so forth. He seems to recognize that there are important differences among people and some room has to be allowed for these practical distinctions. Eventually, after 1,900 years, the Catholic Church rejected slavery among its members; it has not so far admitted that women can reach the same human potential as men: they cannot be ordained.

It would also not be historically correct to claim that the early church developed into an organization marked by fraternity more than hierarchy. Soon enough the early church reverted to the standard kinds of power relationships that prevailed in the ambient society of the time. About the only ones who actually used the term "brother" were the monks, and they often did not seem to realize its full implications. Still, we do come across passages such the whole of Benedict's Chapter 72 (On the Good Zeal) where equality and brotherhood are very much the norm. And we also recall that Benedict himself quotes Galatians 3:28 (at RB 2.20) in his chapter on the abbot.

Certainly, when we are discussing the question of hierarchy in the monastery it is crucial to remember that equality in Christ is a bedrock Christian principle. Anything else, including the hierarchy so beloved of the Catholic Church, is strictly secondary. So even if we find it convenient to say that date of entry and rank are Benedict's "default mode," that is not strictly true. Underlying any such distinctions is our unity in Christ. If the monastery is what it should be, namely, a foretaste of heaven, every effort should be made to emphasize the heavenly condition. Obviously there will be no hierarchical rank in heaven!

But before we cease and desist, let us take one more look at monastic rank. We have already seen that Benedict did not dream up the idea but got it from the earliest cenobitic tradition before him. This in itself indicates that there is probably something about rank that enhances community life. We have seen that Pachomius in southern Egypt already insisted on it, and

Cassian also reports that it was practiced in the monasteries of northern Egypt. There is no reason to suspect that rank disappeared from cenobitic history down through the decades to the time of Benedict.

But of course there is the glaring exception of the Rule of the Master. We really do not know why he abolished rank among his monks, but he did. In this matter he is indeed a radical reformer. And we might cite another obscure clue from the RM to make our point. In his chapter on the abbot the Master has this interesting verse: "Nevertheless, to show his loving kindness to all alike, God commands the elements to serve sinners as much as the just. Therefore let the abbot's charity be the same to all, and let the one discipline be applied to everyone" (RM 2.21-22).

It seems to me that two points could be made here. First, Benedict has omitted these verses. Second, they are apparently based on Matthew 5:45, which insists that the Christian be like the heavenly Father, who "makes his sun rise on the evil and the good, and sends rain on the just and the unjust." So the Master wants the abbot to act the same way, rewarding the bad and the good alike. Note that this is presented as an addendum to the ordinary wisdom that the abbot should reward those monks who are "found better than others in (our) deeds." The Master wants his abbot to go quite beyond the normal ethic of punishment and reward.

Why has Benedict refrained from passing along this apparently high-minded idea from the Master? We cannot be sure why Benedict left it out, because one can never prove a negative. But we must also remember that Benedict knew the whole Rule of the Master, or at least most of it, so he was in a position to see how this kind of extraordinary thinking actually works itself out in the Master's Rule.

At the risk of repeating myself, or even worse of coming across as utterly prejudiced against the poor Master, I would suggest that his basic approach to monastic authority had rather disastrous results. For the Master to exalt the abbot above the ordinary prudence of rewarding the virtuous was simply an excuse for the imposition of despotism. His exempting the abbot from customary constraints such as the reward of virtue had the result of relegating everybody else to a kind of non-status. As it was said of Pharaoh in ancient Egypt, in the Rule of the Master the abbot is the only full human being; all the rest are mere adjuncts of the superior.

I think Benedict wants no part of such an arrangement. He knows that there is an ideal Christian equality as stated in Galatians 3:28: Neither Jew nor Greek, neither slave or free, not male and female. But he also knows that there are real differences among people. Some monks are smarter than others, some monks are more virtuous than others, and so on. Benedict thinks these differences should be acknowledged in the practical arrangements of the monastery. To give a simple example, when it comes to choosing monastic officers such as the deans or the cellarer or the "spiritual seniors" (RB 46.5-6), real merit must be taken into consideration. We need the best people for these jobs.

Somebody with an elementary understanding of political theory can see that this is simply an application of "meritocracy," the system wherein talented and hard-working people are rewarded with important roles in the community. There is nothing especially Christian about such thinking, but it certainly can be *effective*. Unlike societies where other considerations such as age or class status or money determine who achieves positions of influence, in this kind of system there is only interest in who can actually do the job. It is said that among the Plains Indians of the United States as soon as the leader proved he could no longer lead the hunt he was summarily replaced.

Of course, we should not order our communities quite so roughly. But we still need to order them! Like Benedict, we need to give each person his or her *place*, that is, a secure position from which to operate. This need not be seen as sacrosanct status but it should still be seen as the real possession of the individual. It should not be arbitrarily tampered with. Unlike the Master (RM 92.33ff.) we do not "scramble" the communal *statio* on a whim. We do not assign PhDs to slop the hogs to keep them in their place, as was done during the Cultural Revolution in Maoist China. That was a catastrophic blunder that set China back years and years. Benedict wants none of that.

Chapter Seventeen   *Channel Surfing*

Electronic Restlessness

Electronics are among the most significant developments in modern culture, and the mass media they make possible are even more characteristic of our age. Apart from all the other ramifications, the sheer amount of time some people spend with the mass media makes them a huge influence on society. In this chapter I want to explore an aspect of the electronic media that might be labeled "electronic restlessness."

Those of us who do not watch television alone are well aware of the social behavior of other people. With the invention of the remote control one is now in a position to change channels without getting up from one's chair. In fact, you can jump from channel to channel in rapid succession, thereby driving some of your fellow-watchers to distraction or perhaps despair. In a communal setting it is considered very important to keep the clicker *out* of certain hands. Otherwise we could all be in for a very nervous evening.

Of course, there are good reasons for channel surfing. If you are watching a football game and you do not like the ads you simply switch channels for a minute or two and then return to the action. Never mind that you just missed the most significant play of the game; you still were spared the sixth repetition of the obnoxious ad for a forthcoming movie on Home Box Office. And then there are the people who actually *like* the ads. Maybe they prefer the ads to the football. What about them?

Sometimes this scrolling moves to another level altogether. Now we don't just jump channels to avoid things; we do so out of sheer boredom and ennui. The fact that cable gives us at least fifty channels to choose from and the added fact that there is nothing worth watching on most of them most of the time promotes fickleness in the viewer. God help anybody else in the room who happens to want to follow some program through to the end. We are at the mercy of the person with the clicker.

Actually, it seems that television itself promotes this kind of behavior. As is well known, the advertisements are spaced about six minutes apart. Someone with an advanced degree in abnormal psychology has figured out that people tend to get up to go to the kitchen or the bathroom about every six minutes. Therefore the material is broken up into units of that length to accommodate the average attention span of the viewers. But this also tends to shape the psyches of those watching so that gradually, imperceptibly, their attention spans shrink to six minutes.

This conditioning from TV has important repercussions for the rest of life. For example, someone who is faced with teaching a standard college class of fifty minutes has got a major problem on her hands. You can more or less watch the lights go out around the room as you exceed the six-minute attention limit. The creative lecturer knows how to regain the attention of the listeners with a joke or a brief group discussion, but as a society we are much less willing to pay attention to extended discourse than we used to be.

Within TV itself the minuscule attention span has many implications. For example, news broadcasts now avoid any kind of extended discussion. Rather, they go for "sound bites," short, snappy quotations that are meant to catch the attention. What's wrong with that? Nothing, except that some news stories involve fairly complex material that cannot be captured in "sound bites." Anyone who has been interviewed for television knows how frustrating is can be to have a carefully nuanced statement reduced to one short remark that can distort the whole thing.

Somebody like me who has to preach homilies on a fairly regular basis knows that all this very much affects the expectations of the listeners. Even on Sunday, when people used to expect a substantial discourse from the preacher, it is now rather resented if the speaker goes over ten minutes. Years ago, and especially in Protestant churches, the preacher was accused of shirking his duty if he could not produce at least half an hour of commentary on Scripture or doctrine. Nowadays Catholics have become especially critical of anyone who speaks at length in the pulpit.

Granted, it is not just the media that changed all this. In the good old days many people more or less depended on the church to keep them occupied on Sunday. At least in rural parishes the priest might easily talk an hour at Mass. His discourse often included all kinds of peripheral material, and especially world news, since he was often the only well-informed person in the parish. People also came an hour early for catechism for the children, and after lunch, which they ate in the yard, they returned to church for Benediction of the Blessed Sacrament. On Sunday years ago nobody was in a hurry, but now everybody is. Indeed, with all the other activity that takes place on Sunday morning it is often very hard for people to squeeze in a little church. What wonder, then, if they have no wish for any kind of extended oratory?

This is not a nostalgic wish for windiness as such. A lot of it was simply undisciplined blabbing. Every good preacher knows that it is much harder to craft a tight, well-shaped message than a long, rambling one. There is no intrinsic value in wordy services as such. Still, our present-day unwillingness to spend time in church must say something about our faith in general. Recently one of the nearby parishes had to abandon its church building for a year of renovation. The congregation met in a local movie theater and the priest got them out of there in half an hour. People were ecstatic! They were not so happy when the priest resumed his usual fifteen-minute homilies back in church.

To return to our subject, which is general jumpiness, we can see how it has spread to the print media. Have you noticed that the newspapers are getting shorter and shorter? Part of this is an economic crisis in which they cannot afford to print more because their advertising revenue has fallen so much, but I think it also has to do with the feeling that people are no longer much interested in reading long articles. The obvious answer is to give them short ones. But some topics are very hard to reduce to a few inches of newsprint and must be studied in detail to be really understood.

Someone might respond that there is no reason to lament this trend since the print media themselves are doomed. Bitter as it may be for us hard-core readers to swallow, there is some basis to this opinion. Since so much of the news is now available on the Internet, and since more and more people are accustomed to accessing it in that form, the future of the print media does seem to be cloudy. This in itself does not mean that extended material cannot be presented on the computer, but at this point there are also some questions about that.

For example, about fifteen years ago it was announced that someone was working seriously on a weekly news magazine for the Internet. That must have caused *Time* and *Newsweek* to quake in their boots. Yet it never happened. Why? There are conflicting reports, but I think the main reason is that *most people do not like to read a computer screen.* This does not apply to all people, but for many of us the idea of having to sit upright in front of a screen is not a particularly pleasurable experience. It is all right for work, but for pleasure, forget it!

Now there is a handheld computer that can access whole books. A Kindle© or iPad© now enables you to get at hundreds and thousands of books electronically if you are willing to pay for them, and many thousands of others are free. But the question still is whether it is a pleasurable experience. If it is not, then it has no future. Someone has to come up with a screen that looks and feels like the page of a good book, and also how to import good illustrations, maps, and so on. This is a work in progress. Of course we hard-core readers are hard to please, and we are also prejudiced against anything that might replace a book. After all, a book is one of the choicest inventions of the human race.

Before we leave the topic of electronic discourse we should not omit the phenomenon of texting. As most people under thirty know, this involves sending instant messages on a handheld computer. The important aspect of these messages, at least for our discussion here, is that they must be *short*—no more than 140 characters. Such brevity forces people to abbreviate words but, more importantly, it also forces them to make extremely compact statements. And that in turn leads them to think in short bursts. Anybody who doubts that our thinking can be so shaped should try living in a foreign language situation. When you have only a few words and less grammar in a language, the inevitable result is that you speak briefly, but you also tend to cease thinking complex thoughts.

Our general theme in this part is the nervousness and shortened attention-span created by the mass media, and here we run into one of its most serious consequences, namely, "dumbing down." This rather ugly neologism refers to the process of addressing people in increasingly primitive terms for fear they cannot understand complex language and ideas. Certainly one has to be realistic. If you insist on employing language too elevated for your audience you will not be understood or heeded. But the other side of the coin is this: if you condescend too much to the supposed simplicity of people you actually contribute to their degree of obtuseness.

I sometimes find it shocking to encounter old books that seem to make no effort to dumb down their message. Have you ever tried to read the sermons of Jonathan Edwards? Could ordinary churchgoers in western Massachusetts in the eighteenth century possibly have understood such convoluted prose and intricate ideas? Apparently they did, or Edwards would have been fired from his pastorate. Or try reading St. Augustine's sermons to the people of Hippo in the fifth century. How could they have followed such demanding diction for long hours at a time? We don't know. But the point here is that we denizens of the twenty-first century have become unable and unwilling to cope with such stuff. Have our brains shrunk? That is a depressing thought. Let's turn to St. Benedict for some advice.

Read Straight through to the End

> During the days of Lent, in the morning they should be free for their read-
> ings until the end of the third hour, and they are to work until the end
> of the tenth hour at what has been assigned them. In these Lenten days,
> they should each accept a book from the library which they are to read
> straight to the end. These books are to be given out at the beginning of
> Lent. (RB 48.14-16)

In connection with the remarks we have made in the first part, the most
salient remark in this passage from Benedict's chapter on the horarium
is this: "a book which they are to read straight through to the end." We
have been lamenting the decreasing ability of people in our culture to
pursue things "straight through to the end." If you get bored with the TV
program you simply switch channels. Moreover, if you get bored with a
book you can switch books.

In Benedict's time, however, it was seldom as simple as that, because
books were a rare commodity. Compared to our own situation in which
we sometimes feel almost inundated by them, ancient books were anything
but a cheap item. It took weeks and months to copy a book by hand, so it
was a very precious object. Consequently, a well-stocked monastic library
of that time might have a couple hundred books, no more. These books
were few enough that they needed only a chest, not a whole room or a
building, for storage. The chest, called *arca*, was normally kept locked
and the key was in the possession of the sacristan or liturgical master
of ceremonies, called *precentor*. In some monasteries, such as those of
Pachomius in the fourth century, monks were not to keep books in their
private possession overnight. By the time of Benedict things were probably
a bit less constrained. Then monks were allowed to keep a book for a year.

Actually, the text of the Rule does not say that, but we know it was
true at least by the later Middle Ages. We read that at Barking Abbey in
England at the beginning of Lent the nuns were to return the books they
had kept for *lectio* for the past year. As their names (and books) were read
off by the precentor they came forward and placed their book on a special
carpet. Then they were issued another book for the coming year. What is
clear in all this is that the books were highly prized objects that were not
allowed to float around in loose fashion.

This was a disciplined library system, yet it was also different from
our idea of a library. Notice, for example, that Benedict says the monks
are to *accept* a book for Lenten reading. That implies they do not choose
their own book, a thing many of us might find almost unbearable, for one
of the great pleasures of using a library is the opportunity to choose for

yourself what you want to read. I have to admit that my translation of *accipiant* as "accept" is not the usual one. In *Benedict's Rule* I translated it as "receive," which is a different idea. Of course, in both cases one is passive, but "accept" is a more explicit act of the will.

Another change from my own translation of RB 48.15 concerns the rendition of the Latin term *bibliotheca*. In 1996 I translated this word as "Bible," but the usual meaning is "library," as I have given it here. Yet some of the church fathers like Jerome called the Bible itself a *bibliotheca*. They had a point, since the Bible consists of many books written by many different people. Still, "Bible" is a very specialized meaning for *bibliotheca* and is not accepted by most translators of the Rule.

The main reason why some scholars think Benedict may have given out books of the Bible before Lent has to do with *lectio divina* itself. Clearly the early monks closely connected the practice of spiritual reading with the Bible. Those who are wondering how Benedict could have distributed books of the Bible should be advised that ancient handwritten Bibles were normally divided into nine sections. A single handwritten manuscript Bible would have been far too big for personal use, so the various quires were bound separately. Thus the first quire would contain the Pentateuch, the second the historical books, and so on.

The ancient practice of *lectio divina* also differed from our modern habits in other ways. For example, one of the typical monastic exercises was to memorize passages of the Bible rather than merely reading them. This was done in order to stock one's memory bank, as it were, so that such passages could be repeated to oneself throughout the day. The old monks sometimes referred to this as "chewing the cud," a reference to the cow working over the contents of its stomach throughout the day. But in the rest of this paper I would prefer to depart from the specialized meaning of *lectio divina* and concentrate on the more straightforward idea of the monk reading his book "straight through to the end."

When I was in the novitiate the novice master tried to drum many things into our heads. Not much of it stuck in mine, but at least one thing did. He said that Abbot Cuthbert, who was one of his monastic idols, had always told them to read a book all the way to the end and to do it with a pencil in hand. Since the novitiate was a time when reading was my salvation, this comment hit home. I don't agree with the idea of marking up a book, at least if it is not a personal copy. But the part about reading all the way to the end strikes me as very good advice.

Certainly this wisdom saying was not made in a vacuum. It was meant to counteract the common tendency to give up too easily on books and to flit aimlessly from book to book. As I interpret Cuthbert's advice, it implies that a book is a sort of contract. Once you have opened the cover and begun to read there is an obligation to pursue the project to the end. This does not mean one cannot dip into a book at random to see what it is like, nor does it mean one must read only one book at a time. Personally I find it helpful sometimes to move from book to book in order to keep my mind fresh. After all, some books are tough going and one does need a change of pace.

I also assume that Abbot Cuthbert was not talking about recreational reading. No one needs to urge us to finish a delightful murder mystery or something else that provides relaxation. Moreover, I can't see that anyone is likely to have a problem finishing such a book. But we are talking here about serious reading, the kind that really should be classified as work, and the same rules apply to it as to any kind of responsible approach to work. When you begin a job the adult thing is to finish it. It is a sign of immaturity to begin book after book without completing them.

Why should we finish the books we begin? For one thing, you never really know what is in a book until you finish it. Granted, the first pages probably will give you a fairly good impression of the author's style and also the significance of the theme. But some authors take a while to get going; if you give up on them too soon you can miss a lot. This is probably a weakness in a writer, but still the reader has to take her as he finds her. From experience I can say that some books take a long time to build up steam, but they pay abundant rewards to the patient, even dogged reader who refuses to give up. "He who perseveres until the end will be saved."

But aren't some books just about impossible to read? Of course they are, at least for a given reader. This is plainly a personal question. Some writers just do not suit some readers. Since I am stubborn and almost fanatical about doing serious reading I rarely give up on a book. But now and then, maybe once a year, I do. For example, try as I might I could never get more than a few pages into Hans Urs von Balthasar's book called *Prayer*. He is a famous spiritual author and that book is often quoted by estimable people, but I cannot read it. I cannot read Elias Canetti's *Crowds*, either, but that is another story.

What about books that are in a sort of twilight zone? I refer to important books one "should" read, but that are not quite penetrable. In my own case this applies to many works of theology but almost *all* works of philosophy. I can just about understand them, but not quite. Is there any profit in such reading? I think there is. You might call this "standing on your tiptoes" as you read. It can be very hard work, and it can also be irritating, but it probably helps one to move to a slightly deeper level of comprehension. I am not talking now about *Finnegan's Wake*, of which

I can hardly decipher one single word. I mean reading that is just a little beyond me. I think it is worth pursuing.

Moreover, it seems to me that this kind of serious reading is good for monks. Of course it is probably good for anyone with ordinary intellectual curiosity. But St. Benedict has arranged for a considerable amount of the daily schedule to be devoted to *lectio divina*. Indeed, he sets aside no less than three full hours at the beginning of each Lenten day for such activity. For most people the first three hours of the morning are prime time for intellectual work, so it is pretty evident that Benedict thinks it should be spent in a serious fashion. Certainly it is not for recreational reading!

If this appears to the casual reader to be a fairly obvious matter, then be assured that for most monks it is not! Of course, there are many ways to observe Benedict's horarium. But one of the most difficult aspects of that daily schedule in most monasteries is precisely the arrangement for reading. To put the matter bluntly, very few monks in our modern world have three hours for daily *lectio divina*. In fact, few of them even have a single hour of prime reading time when they are at their best and can cope with really serious spiritual literature.

This does not mean that few monks are readers! In fact, most of them have to do a great deal of reading every day. But by and large it is utilitarian reading, material they need to get through in connection with their jobs. Very often this means doing background reading for their classes, and a lot of this is heavy material. But it is not what Benedict would classify as *lectio divina*. He is talking about reading for *formation*, not for information. Yet it cannot be denied that there is no clear-cut line of demarcation between the two. For example, the priest who must prepare a sermon is also nourishing himself spiritually. Yet today many monks find themselves in work situations in which they must deal with endless memos and policy statements and such stuff. Since modern monastic life can become very complex there is no alternative to reading this kind of material. But it can hardly be described as nourishment for the soul.

Some years ago a well-known monastic writer remarked to me that there was a notable difference between the old lay brothers and the younger ones. He said: "The old brothers practiced a trade and they read books. The young ones are vice-presidents and they read magazines." Since the old brothers are mostly dead and departed, only the young brothers might happen to read this comment. It could seem hurtful and unfair to them, especially since they are doing their work out of obedience. As for a trade, it is almost a luxury for a modern monk to be able to work with his hands at some skilled occupation. Not all the old brothers pursued the kind of idyllic life this scholar seemed to imagine. After all, there have always been "blue-collar" monks who greatly prefer active physical work to paperwork. Benedict himself had those types in his community, and he showed them great respect. He said that if they would not or could not read even on Sunday they should be given some manual labor to do (RB 48.23).

It seems to me, though, that my friend's comment is still well worth examining. Since many monks now find themselves doing middle-level clerical work, the kind that is filled with endless trivial detail, they should beware that this does not spill over into their private "monastic" life. It is very easy in our culture to immerse oneself in trivia even apart from work. Very few monasteries, apart from maybe the Trappists and the Carthusians, make much attempt to shield their monks from the blizzard of popular print culture and television and the Internet. The problem with a lot of this material is not that it is evil but that it is banal and ephemeral. The difficulty I have with *CNN*, *USA Today*, *People*, and the other media of that type is that they skate on the surface and never achieve any depth.

To warn monks away from this kind of superficial material is not to say that we should pursue a narrowly "spiritual" reading list. Monks are responsible adults, and as such they should know what is really going on in the world. Therefore it behooves us to read widely and deeply. In this matter we monks usually have a distinct advantage over other people because most monastic libraries are well stocked with good books on history, politics, and so forth. Even if we live in a small or impoverished monastery that lacks a decent library we are rarely far away from a public library. In other words, there is really no excuse for a monk nowadays to neglect serious reading for want of books.

If there is no shortage of books for us, we still need to develop good habits and techniques to keep us reading. One of the methods that has helped me over the years is the practice of keeping a list of what I have read, and also writing a short summary or response for every book. This book report is not long or detailed. In fact, it is not at all easy to sum up some books. But if the reader attempts to write a few sentences of personal reaction to the book it helps to fix the book in one's memory. If you plow through a lot of books as I do there is a danger of them all running together in the memory. A short, clear record helps to avoid this problem.

Still, there is one aspect of such book lists that ought to be avoided. Do not just chalk up book titles! Some years ago a Benedictine elder confided to an interviewer that he had read twenty thousand books in his long life. I sat down and figured out how many books a year that meant for him, and I concluded that such numbers are hardly possible. But even if they were I would worry that the occupational hazard of such lists is sheer quantity. In the matter of reading, and especially *lectio divina*, quantity is of no interest at all. Speed reading may be possible, but for many of us it is a formula for disaster. Frankly, most important spiritual texts only disclose themselves to a slow, contemplative reader. That is of the very nature of a serious book.

To engage in *lectio divina* we have to calm down and forget a lot of the habits and attitudes we have learned from the mass media. They furnish a psychic babysitter for many people, but for the monk *lectio divina* should be a brush with the holiness of God.